instant **expert** • instant **expert** • instant **expert** • instant **expert** •

# QUILTING

instant **expert** • instant **expert** • instant **expert** •

MQ Publications Limited
12 The Ivories, 6–8 Northampton Street
London N1 2HY
Tel: +44 (0) 20 7359 2244
Fax: +44 (0) 20 7359 1616
email: mail@mqpublications.com
www.mqpublications.com

Illustrator: Penny Brown
Cover Photographer: Sandra Lousada

ISBN: 1-84072-983-X

Printed and bound in China
1 2 3 4 5 08 07 06 05 04

expert • instant **expert** • instant **expert** • instant

# QUILTING

Jenni Dobson

MQP

# Contents

**Left:** Detail of *Basket of Chips*, American, ca. 1920.

# INTRODUCTION

It is with pleasure that in this new century I can write an opening for a collection about quilt-making. It is both a craft and an art. The fact that it is alive and well is due partly to the timeless nature of its appeal and partly to the enthusiasm of existing practitioners. Its survival in the future will become the responsibility of those learning its attractions and satisfactions now—among whom, I hope, will be the readers of this book.

Within the pages is a wealth of creative techniques with something to suit everyone from the patient lover of handwork to the busy stitcher dedicated to the sewing machine. Advice on the basic skills of making a quilt is followed by introductory lessons on a variety of patchwork, appliqué, and quilting methods. Having tried a new technique, in many cases there follows a project for you to hone your new skills. Even as you improve in knowledge and confidence, this book can remain on hand as a reference and reminder.

The quilt-maker of today has an abundance of benefits not available in the past. We no longer have to make do with one color of quilting thread, use up every minute morsel of fabric in order to keep warm, hand sew by candlelight, nor labor with pencil and scissors—unless we choose to. Instead, the range of thread for hand and machine sewing is tremendous, our fabric stores offer a breathtaking collection of new designs every season, and we have arguably more tools than we are likely to need, tempting us to invest in them!

Perhaps the greatest benefit of them all is that most of us have the freedom to make whatever we like, unrestrained by the need simply to keep ourselves and our families warm and clothed. Quilt-making today is more often about decoration for the joy of it and about self-expression in a way that our ancestors might never have dreamed possible.

Yet in one way at least we have something in common with quilters from the past—it is the way that one becomes hooked on this activity. The satisfaction that derives from finishing the latest project and sharing it with like-minded others would be recognized by any of yesterday's quilters. So come on—join us.

**Right:** Detail of *Rose Wreath*, American, early twentieth century.

# A HISTORY OF QUILTING

Today many people comment upon global interest in quilting, as if this is something new. In fact, any student of its history soon realizes that it has been a worldwide activity for a very long time. What has changed is the rate at which new ideas can spread. Instead of mere word of mouth and the slow distribution of goods, with the ideas they communicate, by pack animals or by sea, now books and magazines can spread new trends by airmail, enthusiasts can visit exhibitions on the other side of the world, and even the homebound can enjoy almost instant information via the Internet.

It is unlikely that we shall ever know when the first patch was put onto something to cover a hole, or where, having done that, it was realized that such a patch could be applied to be decorative. Nor shall we know who it was that decided if a single layer wasn't warm enough, extra padding might be better. Yet from such humble beginnings, probably spontaneously in more than one place, the whole glorious art and craft that is quilting, derives. The following pages highlight some of the curious and noteworthy stages in this history.

**Left:** Detail of *Variable Star*, American, early nineteenth century.

# A BRIEF HISTORY OF QUILT-MAKING

Let's begin with a few definitions. A quilt is generally considered to be made with three layers: a top, some filling, termed batting, and a backing. Quilting is the stitching that holds these layers together, being both practical and almost invariably decorative. Today a quilt might just as easily be made to hang on a wall as to lie on a bed. Quilting has also been used for centuries on clothing. Indeed some of our best evidence for quilting in the past comes from the survival of such garments.

The top layer of a quilt may be composed of a single piece or two or three large pieces of fabric where the interest results mainly from the quilting patterns. This type of quilt is called "wholecloth."

Alternatively, the top layer can be pieced from a collection of fabrics, coordinated or otherwise, in a variety of patterns, highly organized or random, and then it is described as patchwork. Here, the overall impact results from the patchwork with the quilting often of secondary importance. Between these two styles is a third which is made from moderately large areas of fabric pieced into a simple pattern, such as seven or nine strips, known as a "strippy," or a square of fabric on point inside a larger frame. The quilting generally takes pride of place on these simple shapes.

A further method uses patches of cloth sewn to a base fabric, either in units or large panels, to form motifs in a technique known as appliqué.

Not all bedspreads made with either patchwork or appliqué contain the filling needed to earn the term "quilt." They may be simply backed with cloth with minimal stitching to keep the two layers together. Quilt historians generally term these items coverlets, or bedspreads.

The earliest surviving example of a textile that we would recognize as a quilt was found in a tomb near the Mongolian-Siberian border, southwest of Lake Baikal and is now in Russia. Believed to date from between 100 BC and AD 200, it shows couched embroidery, spirals, and diamond crosshatching. Just a little younger is a patchwork altar valance of rare yet still colorful Tang dynasty silks, preserved by the extremely dry conditions of the cave on the Silk Route where it was found in the early twentieth century. This is thought to date from the eighth or ninth century and is in the British Museum (Stein collection), London.

From *The Travels of Marco Polo*, written around the end of the thirteenth century, about his journey to China that commenced in 1271, we can glean evidence about quilting. Discussing crops that are found in India, he says:

"There is also plenty of cotton, for the cotton trees grow here to a great height—as much as six paces after twenty years growth. But when they reach this age they no longer produce cotton fit for spinning, but only for use in wadding or padded quilts."

This suggests that the use of cotton fibers as filling for quilts was well established and also not unfamiliar, or he would have needed to explain the practice at more length for the understanding of his readers.

**Left:** English medallion, American, early nineteenth century.
**Right:** Detail of *Mariner's Compass*, American, early twentieth century.

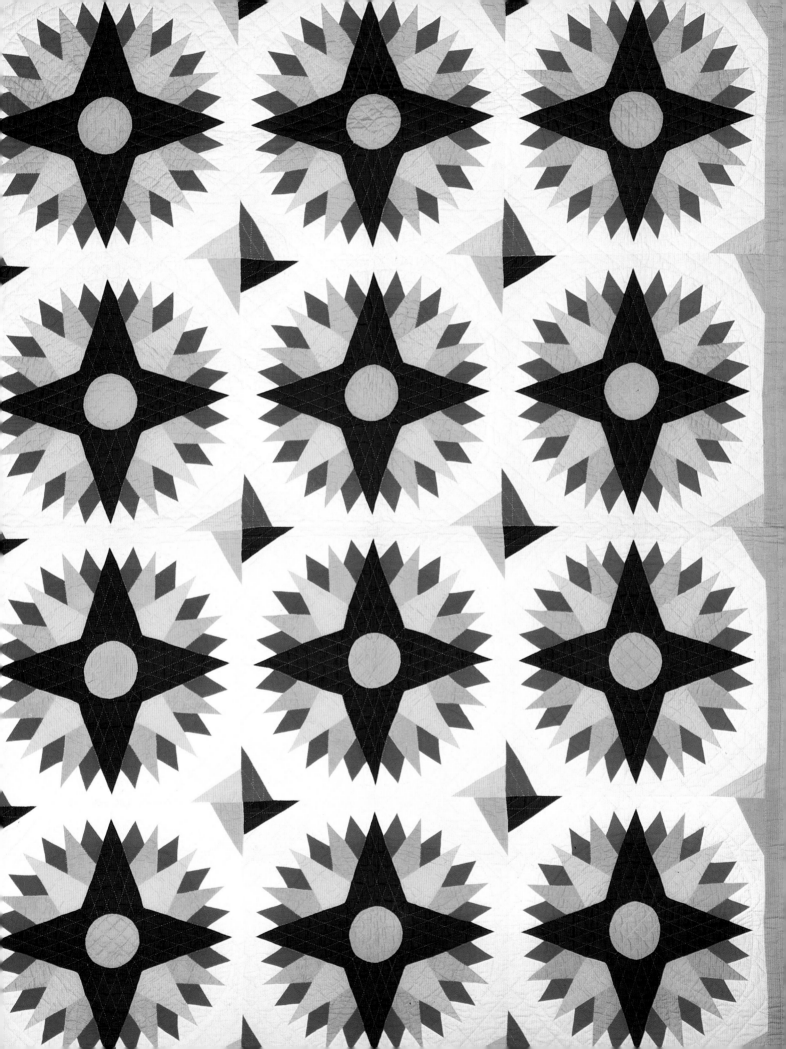

**Above:** Silk patchwork coverlet, English, 1718, the earliest known dated bedspread.

Dating from about a century later, three Sicilian quilts are well documented. Two of them were made as a pair, one of which is in the Bargello, Florence, and the third is in the Victoria and Albert Museum, London. The latter is complete, being worked with backstitch on two layers of heavy linen. The motifs are filled with cotton padding, a technique known as "stuffed quilting." This method of working without batting throughout the whole and instead inserting fillings into enclosed shapes has continued throughout history, e.g., in the French tradition known as "boutis."

Costume researchers using sources such as sculpture and manuscripts know that in the Middle Ages quilting was widely used for garments and not only for warmth: soldiers were protected in battle by tunics with stitched parallel channels. These were filled with whatever was on hand including straw or wooden strips. Knights would have quilted vests to protect them from their chain mail, or armor.

Nevertheless, in the often drafty houses that previous generations of Europeans inhabited, quilted clothing must have been welcomed for its warmth. Examples survive of women's and men's jackets and vests but perhaps most well known are the quilted petticoats. Numerous other small items can be seen in museums including caps and bonnets for adults, as well as charming versions for babies and children. The detail with which family portraits were rendered at a time before photography suggests that quilting on clothing existed right through from Tudor to Victorian times, though with variations in style and popularity. Family archives also show that there were workshops in cities like London from which custom-made sets of quilted clothing could be ordered.

Returning to the quilt as bedspread, it seems that wholecloth may be the most long-standing tradition. If so, then it appears to have been a logical small step toward the appliqué quilt which made use of every precious scrap of the expensive prints when they began to be imported from the Far East. Motifs were carefully cut out and sewn to the background fabric in a style that became known as "appliqué perse." Fine examples of this work exist in countries such as Britain and the Netherlands, which both had powerful trading networks. Even by the turn of the eighteenth century, such fabrics were becoming more widely available as shown by surviving quilts made from a piece of printed chintz, quilted around the motifs.

In turn, the expansion of Britain and Europe into colonies resulted in lucrative trade with the colonists. Even though the origins of patchwork are lost in the mists of time, it was probably the high cost of fabric that ensured its continuation.

Three broad approaches to patchwork can be defined. One is the use of a single shape that tessellates over the entire surface. The hexagon is arguably the most common as it is reasonably simple to draft but various other shapes can be used or combined together. The effect created resembles that of mosaic tiles. A particular working method for tessellated designs, of basting fabric over precisely cut templates then oversewing them invisibly together, has become known as "English paper-piecing," but examples can be found in France, the Netherlands, and Sweden, to name but three others.

A version of this method was used by the maker of the 1718 coverlet (seen opposite), now in the collection of the Quilters' Guild of the British Isles. Important as the earliest known dated English patchwork, this features many motifs that modern makers would work in appliqué but all were pieced over stiff paper, including the date and maker's initials, "E. H." The silks used are surprisingly colorful. Two of the fabrics could have been one hundred years old at the time they were included in the quilt. All of them were produced at a time when spinning of yarn and weaving of cloth were done by hand.

A second approach produces the "frame," or medallion quilt, which is constructed from successive "frames," or borders, built up around a central medallion. This might be a focal point of patchwork, appliqué, or a printed panel. The frames might vary in width or pattern. This strategy suits both the person who prefers to plan toward a specific goal and the one who will simply build up circuits of patchwork until a useful size is reached. It is fairly common to find extra rows of pattern added to the top and bottom to form a rectangular rather than square end product.

The third approach focuses on the working of separate units known as blocks, most often but not exclusively square in shape. These can be pieced or appliquéd. When sufficient blocks have been worked, they are sewn together, either directly or with strips of fabric between, which may also be pieced, to form a top. This in turn can be enlarged or the design developed by the addition of a border. Block production means that if a mistake occurs, a single unit can be discarded without compromising the final whole, but it offers another major benefit—portability. Perhaps for this reason the block method of construction became highly popular in the United States. Immigrants from many European countries arrived with their own traditions of sewing, yet most seem to have found in the block both convenience and potential. The number of ways that a simple square can be pieced is endless, and evocative names assigned to those patterns reflect the life and locality of the makers.

**Above:** *Nine-patch,* American, early nineteenth century.

The distinctive exception can be seen in the quilts of the Amish community, which has become known for working in strong solid, i.e., not printed, colors and with bold designs that frequently do not use blocks. Appliqué is extremely rare, being thought nonessential, and it is quilting that contributes the most decorative element. Amish quilts bear a strong resemblance to those of Welsh origin and historians have begun to consider the possibility of cross-fertilization of ideas between these two communities, who settled the same parts of the United States and shared fairly compatible religious beliefs.

Whichever construction is used, patchwork can be executed in either a carefully devised color scheme or from a collection of scraps. The scrap quilt has become a genre in its own right. When skillfully arranged, it presents a feast for the eyes and a tour de force of vision on the part of the maker. It frequently adds charm and nostalgia to these qualities, as the maker often knows exactly where the scraps originated and associates them with people, places, or events. At the other end, even the most ramshackle collection of scraps has the power to cheer and keep warm the poor or needy, as proved by the number of goodwill or charity projects engaged in by quilt-makers almost everywhere.

The coming of industrialization caused a surge in textile production. In 1767, James Hargreaves invented the "spinning jenny," and, in 1771, Sir Richard Arkwright used water to drive spinning machines. Soon steam was driving

banks of spinning mules and power looms while roller-printing revolutionized the affordability of patterned cloth. Fabrics were more widely available than ever before and at prices that more people could afford. Yet scrap quilts continued to be made, even by those who could afford to do otherwise, and this must be due to their visual appeal and potential for diversity. A quilt made from a collection of printed cottons has a very different character from that of a Victorian Crazy, rich with silk and velvet dressmaker's scraps and heavily embellished with embroidery.

The migration of populations, such as the Scots displaced by the Enclosures Act, or later the Irish by potato famines, and any number of persecuted religious groups, contributed to the international nature of patchwork and quilting. These ordinary people carried with them the skills they already had and which were desperately needed, whether starting a new life in America or Australia. In addition, from the nineteenth century onward, missionaries from Europe and the United States traveled to far-flung destinations, and along with Christianity, taught the sewing skills with which they were familiar. Today, their influence can be seen in both working methods and subject matter.

Of course, not all missionaries needed to travel far. Those engaged in "saving the souls" of African slaves on American plantations also played their part, as can be seen in the two wonderful "story" quilts by the former slave

**Above:** *One-patch with Needlepoint,* Welsh, 1915.

Harriet Powers of Georgia. This was Harriet's name for them but their style typifies a form that became associated with African Americans. Students of ethnic art see characteristics of African culture intermingled with those of a Western or European tradition in this style of quilt-making.

Harriet's quilts belong to what today are known as Bible quilts. The making of such quilts must once have been more common than we might imagine because printed panels were produced of important quotations from the Bible. This would not have been commercially viable unless more were made than the few surviving examples might suggest. Most likely they just wore out, having been made as "good works" for the needy.

Sewing was often taught as a means of improvement to the disadvantaged, such as prisoners. Elizabeth Fry, a reformer of prisons in Great Britain, is perhaps the most well-known member of a group that, until 1841, supplied British convict women being transported to Australia with a bag of useful things including two pounds of patch-work pieces. The idea was that they would have a task to employ them on the voyage, and upon arrival, either something to sell or make use of themselves. An example, found in Scotland in the 1980s, was sent back to Britain, with a message of gratitude, presumably soon after it was made. It is now in the National Gallery of Australia, Canberra.

In the second half of the nineteenth century, the invention of the sewing machine offered the possibility of new ways to work, besides speeding up the task. A "loss leader" style campaign by one manufacturer that gave sewing machines free to ministers' wives in the developing communities of the United States, fostered the social desirability of machines, and hence increased sales.

Arriving at the twentieth century, these strands were all still present. Technology still fed the demands of makers on the plus side, while on the down side, hardship, particularly the Depression, still kept alive the traditions of making do and using scraps. Tops from the Depression years in the United States reveal just how thin the fabric might be, even in the bright new colors popularized by the Art Deco style. In Britain, women in Wales and northeast England earned a few shillings by making quilts to order. In Australia, shortages produced the "wagga," made from whatever was on hand, including sometimes even knitted panels, and filled with recycled materials.

The role of quilt-making for public good is worthy of study by itself. In many communities quilts were made directly for those in need or as a way of raising money. Examples include signature quilts, where folk paid to

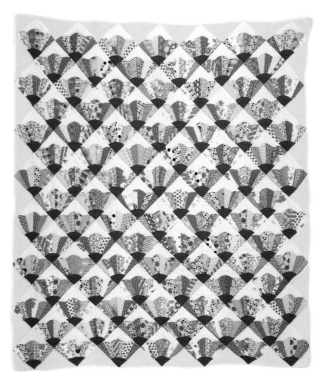

**Above:** Fans quilt, American, early twentieth century.

sign their names on a square of cotton, which were then embroidered, assembled, and raffled. One such exists where I live in England, made to complete the local memorial for World War I. During World War II, Canadians sent packages of quilts via the Red Cross for the victims of bombing in Great Britain, several of which survive in the collection of the Quilters' Guild.

Perhaps due to associations with poverty, patchwork and quilting had reduced in popularity in the postwar years. Then in the late 1970s, the Americans celebrated their bicentennial and a landmark exhibition of their quilts went on an international tour. Suddenly, quilt-making was rediscovered as a thing of beauty and creative potential—and here we are today.

Not only are new people being drawn to learning quilting, but more status is being afforded to quilts as makers venture increasingly into the world of art. Several countries have undertaken documentation projects to record the artifacts owned by private individuals. More study is being made not just of the antique quilts that survive but also of the materials from which they were made and the social conditions of their makers. Meanwhile, besides making for their own families and for pleasure, quilters continue to invest their time and talents benefiting, among others, neonatal units, battered wives, children in Eastern European orphanages, and victims of flood, fire, and hurricanes around the world.

# THE BASICS

This section offers all the essential definitions, skills, and techniques needed for quilt-making. Whether you wish to sew by hand or by machine, you will find simple instructions to cover all approaches to choosing equipment, cutting, piecing, appliquéing, pressing, quilt assembling, layering, and finishing.

Working through the key stages set out in this section is just like taking a series of classes with a teacher. By the end of this section, you will be familiar with commonly used terms and processes. This methodical approach will enable you to take on the techniques described in later sections of the book.

Try to complete each stage as well as possible but do not be too critical—it is better to experience the pleasure of finishing a project and feeling motivated to start another than to set such high standards for yourself that you never finish anything.

**Left:** Detail of *Maple Leaf*, American, ca. 1880.

# GETTING TO KNOW YOUR QUILT

A quilt is made up of three layers of fabric: a decorative top, a middle lining, and a backing, known together as the "quilt sandwich." The layers are held together with a decorative running stitch, the quilting, or by a simpler method, such as tying.

## 1 Quilt Top
The upper layer of the quilt sandwich. The top can be pieced, appliquéd, or cut as a single piece of fabric.

## 2 Batting
The middle layer, or the "filling" in a quilt. It can be made of cotton, wool, silk, or synthetic fibers (page 158).

## 3 Backing
The bottom layer of the quilt sandwich.

## 4 Block
A single design unit that when sewn together with other blocks creates the quilt top. A block can be any shape and can be pieced, plain, or appliquéd.

## 5 Pieced Block
A single design unit of several smaller units or pieces.

## 6 Alternate Block
A plain square used in the design to contrast and alternate with pieced or appliquéd blocks.

## 7 Sashing/Setting Strips
Strips of fabric used to join blocks.

## 8 Sashing Square/Cornerstone
A square of fabric that joins sashing to sashing at the intersection of the component blocks.

## 9 On-point Block
A block turned on its corner to read as a diamond.

## 10 Corner Triangle
A triangle cut with the straight grain around the right-angle corner and used to square up blocks on-point.

## 11 Side Triangle
A triangle with the straight grain down the long side and used to fill in between blocks on-point.

## 12 Appliqué Block
A block made by sewing fabric shapes onto a background, either by hand or by machine. Usually representational.

## 13 Sashing/Lattice Strips
Narrow strips of fabric sewn around all four sides of a block like a picture frame. Their function is to clarify the design, enlarge blocks, and stabilize the edges of a complex piecing design.

## 14 Inner Border
An internal frame of fabric designed to draw together the various central motifs. This device is often used with pieced outer borders.

## 15 Mitered Corner
A corner finished by sewing the fabric strips at a 45° angle (pages 42–3).

## 16 Straight-cut Corner
A corner finished by sewing strips at right angles (page 43).

## 17 Outer Border
A frame sewn around the top unifying the design. Borders can be narrow, wide, plain, pieced, or appliquéd (page 40).

## 18 Pieced Border
A decorative border made up of various fabric pieces.

## 19 Appliqué Border
Often used as a decorative complement to an appliquéd quilt top.

## 20 Corner Block or Post
A square that joins the horizontal and vertical border strips.

## 21 Rounded Corner
An alternative to square corners requiring the use of bias binding.

## 22 Quilting
A decorative running stitch sewn by hand or machine that holds the three layers of the quilt together (page 156).

## 23 Binding
A narrow fabric strip used to finish the raw edges of a quilt (page 48).

# EQUIPMENT

It is helpful to remember that quilts can be made with the simplest of tools. In the past, magnificent quilts were made using only needles, pins, scissors, a pencil, and a ruler. There are lots of tempting goodies available at quilting supply stores; part of your progression from beginner to experienced quilt-maker will include discovering which of those are most useful. As a rule, buy the best tools you can afford.

## Needles

Needles are sold in packets of mixed sizes or all of one size. For a beginner, mixed packets are most useful. Experiment with different sizes on various fabrics to discover what works best.

For hand piecing, hand appliqué, and finishing bindings, use "sharps." They are moderately long, with some flexibility and an easy-to-thread eye. For exceptionally fine work, some quilters like to use embroidery or crewel needles.

Use "betweens" for quilting. They are shorter and have less flexibility. If you are a beginner, start with a larger-size needle and progress to a smaller one as you gain experience.

Large, long needles such as darning needles, "straws," and even doll-making needles, are useful for basting the quilt layers together.

## Pins

Buy good-quality pins. Do not use burred or rusted pins, or reuse pins from packaging, as they will mark your fabric. Use long pins with ball or plastic heads rather than dressmaker's pins—they are easier to push through the fabric.

Extra-long pins are available for assembling the quilt layers. Safety pins (size 2) also can be used for basting. For appliqué, use ½-inch or ¾-inch sequin pins to hold little shapes in place.

## Thimbles

Many quilters sew successfully without a thimble, but learning to use one will definitely reduce the likelihood of sore fingers when quilting. A thimble should fit snugly on the finger that you use to push the needle through the fabric. To help keep the thimble on, moisten your fingertip before putting it on. A good tip for beginners is to wear the thimble continuously until it feels like a "second skin."

Thimbles come in metal, plastic, wood, or leather and include the open-ended type, where the user pushes the needle with the side of the finger. Others have a slight ridge around the top to prevent the needle from slipping off the end.

There are thimble substitutes, such as tape or patches of plastic, for those who cannot keep a conventional thimble on their finger.

## Scissors

A good pair of sharp dressmaker's shears is essential for cutting fabrics accurately and should be reserved for cutting fabric only. When choosing scissors, always test the balance and try them for comfort. Poorly balanced or uncomfortable scissors will make your hands ache quickly.

Have another pair of scissors for cutting paper and plastic templates. Use a pair of small embroidery scissors with very sharp points for fine appliqué work, trimming threads, and clipping seam allowances. Specialty scissors are available for reverse appliqué.

## Template-making Equipment

To make templates you will need cardboard or template plastic, a pencil or fine marker, and a ruler or straightedge. Use template plastic rather than cardboard if the template will be used repeatedly.

To cut the shapes, use scissors or a craft knife, which gives more precise results. Always use your craft knife with a metal-edge ruler. To draft original designs, you may also need a set square and a pair of compasses.

## Rotary Cutting Equipment

For quick and accurate cutting, use a rotary cutter along with a self-healing cutting mat and a thick plastic, see-through ruler. Large cutters can slice through up to eight layers of fabric; smaller ones are useful for cutting curves and small pieces. All cutters are fitted with a safety guard because the blades are very sharp. Never use the cutter on any surface other than a self-healing mat, as anything else will quickly blunt the blade.

Cutting mats come in various sizes. A large mat allows you to cut much larger pieces of fabric and removes the need to handle and fold the fabric as often. Small mats are ideal for transporting to classes. Many quilters find that owning more than one mat is the answer. Mats are

Craft Knife

Rotary Cutter

Self-healing Cutting Mat

Tape Measure

Masking Tape

Plastic Templates

Fabric Shears

Safety Pins

Chalk Holder

Embroidery Scissors

Plastic Cutting Ruler

Template Suction Handle

Marking Pencil

Beeswax

Water-Soluble Marker

Ball-headed Pins

Silver Marking Pencil

Sequin Pins

Extra long Pins

Fabric Eraser

Thimbles

generally marked with a grid to help cut bigger pieces of fabric and for lining up the edges of the fabric.

Use a heavy-duty, see-through plastic ruler with your rotary cutter. Choose either a 6 x 24-inch or 3 x 18-inch ruler that is marked in inches, quarter inches, and eighth inches, and 30°, 45°, and 60° angles. Before buying a ruler, place it over assorted printed fabrics to check that the measurements can be read easily.

In addition to basic rulers, there is also a wide variety of rulers for cutting specific shapes, which are, in effect, like multisize templates. Often, these are designed for a particular piecing technique.

## Specialty Equipment

**Bias Bars** Reusable metal strips are useful when long lengths of bias strips of a consistent appearance are needed—for instance, when working stained-glass appliqué or Celtic designs.

**Creative Grid** A 44-inch-wide flannel printed with a 2-inch grid mounted on a wall or foam board makes an ideal design wall.

**Cut-and-press Board** A rotary cutting mat on one side and a padded pressing surface on the other. These are available in several sizes.

**Hot Pen** Device for cutting template shapes from sheets of durable plastic.

**Multisize Plastic Templates** Suitable for use with a rotary cutter, these templates allow you to cut many different sizes of one specific shape.

**Quick Stripper** Adjustable cutter that slices two sets of strips, from 1 inch to 6 inches wide, at once.

**Rotary Blade Sharpener** Easy appliance to use for restoring the edge of the cutter blade.

**Specialty Rulers** These rulers, intended for use with more challenging designs, such as wedges and logs for pineapple patterns, are a time-saving device for all quilters.

**Stencil Cutting Knife** This knife is useful for cutting templates and parallel channels in quilting stencils.

## Iron

Pressing is essential to accurate piecing, and your iron and ironing board should be kept close to your work. Using a steam iron will help set seams.

Travel irons are popular for classes, and they can be set up right beside your sewing machine for easy pressing between stages. Similarly, a small ironing pad or fabric board wrapped in a towel can serve as a portable pressing surface.

## Marking Equipment

For marking seam allowances, tracing around templates, or marking a quilting design, always use a nonpermanent marker. An ordinary well-sharpened graphite pencil is suitable for marking most fabrics. For dark fabrics, where pencil marks cannot easily be read, use colored, air-, or water-soluble markers, a chalk wheel, a sharpened sliver of hard-dried soap, or a pencil with white or silver-gray lead.

If you prefer not to "draw" on your quilt top, other marking methods include masking tape (for geometric designs only), adhesive plastic templates, or a hera marker, a Japanese marking tool that lightly scores the design onto the fabric.

Only use permanent markers for writing quilt labels or drawing in details on appliqué.

Unwanted pencil marks can be removed without damaging the fabric with a special fabric eraser.

## Yardstick

Use a yardstick with a triangle to straighten the edges of each of your fabric pieces.

## Measuring Tape

Use a 120-inch quilt-maker's tape rather than the regular dressmaker's tape, which measures only 60 inches long.

## Thread

Always use good-quality thread for all your work. A 100 percent cotton or cotton-covered polyester is most suitable for hand and machine piecing and appliqué. Choose a color that matches your fabric. Use only dark thread when sewing dark fabrics because any ends of dark thread will show through adjacent lighter fabrics in the finished quilt. When sewing different colors and patterns together, choose a medium to light neutral thread, such as gray or ecru. As an alternative, use "invisible," or monofilament, nylon thread.

● For both machine and hand quilting, use a coated or prewaxed quilting thread. It is stronger than regular sewing thread, and the coating allows it to glide through the quilt layers. If you use regular sewing cotton for quilting, try running your thread lightly across some beeswax.

● Hand quilting can be worked with other special threads, such as pearl or crochet cotton.

● For tying, use embroidery thread, pearl cotton, or crochet cotton.

● For basting, choose a light-colored thread. If you decide to use an inferior-quality basting thread, tiny fibers may shed when the thread is pulled through the fabric.

● Store your spools in a dust-proof container away from direct sunlight.

## Sewing Machine

Although many quilters enjoy handwork, most would agree that a sewing machine is high on the equipment list. Determine which functions you need most and choose a machine accordingly. It is not necessary to have the most expensive model to produce good work. Computerized machines may take longer to use efficiently and can be more costly to repair if anything goes wrong.

Talk to the sales assistants and buy from a supplier willing to offer support and service. Ask to read the machine manual to see how easy it is to follow. Inquire whether classes are available to help you get the most out of your machine. Find out if extra fittings and attachments, such as darning or walking (even-feed) feet, are available and what each one costs.

For traveling to classes, portability and the weight of your machine should be taken into consideration.

## Using Your Sewing Machine

❶ Check that the machine is clean and put in a new needle for each new project. A size 80/12 needle is suitable for most quilt-making tasks.

❷ Thread your machine with the same-weight thread for both the needle and bobbin. To save time when sewing large projects, wind two bobbins.

❸ Check the tension for each project by sewing together two fabrics from the project. The top thread and the lower thread should lock together between the two fabric layers.

If the needle thread is pulled through to the lower side, this means the top tension is too loose.

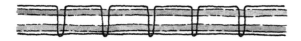

If the bobbin thread is pulled to the top of the work, then the needle (or top) tension is too tight.

Check the overall appearance of the seam. Again, if the fabric puckers, the tension is too tight.

❹ Care for your machine as directed in the manual. Note that some computerized machines can only be professionally serviced. Keep all magnetic items well away from computerized machines.

❺ Take care to remove all fragments when a needle is broken. Safely dispose of damaged or broken needles.

# FABRIC AND COLOR

Fabric is the heart of quilt-making, and manipulating its color and pattern is one of the great joys of patchwork. Once bitten by the quilting bug, quilt-makers become compulsive purchasers of fabric, and having a beautiful collection that includes all the colors of the rainbow is almost as pleasurable as finishing their first quilt.

Often, the basic color for a quilt is predetermined; it is choosing the colors to go with it that causes quilters the most anxiety. A design worked with different fabrics can yield distinctly different results. A fascinating exercise is to make up the same block using a variety of different fabrics and to observe how the placement of color and pattern can affect the block's final appearance. It is important to choose fabrics that harmonize without becoming bland. Choose colors and patterns you like and will enjoy working with. Your fabric collection will grow with each quilt you make, and you should aim to put together a complete palette of colors and values (value is the degree of lightness or darkness of a color). Having a good selection of fabrics from across the color spectrum allows you to make more interesting choices. Sometimes small amounts of the most unlikely color or color value enhance an otherwise predictable scheme.

By arranging your color values in a certain way you can make some areas of your quilt recede and others advance. Light colors seem to advance and attract attention while dark colors appear to recede. This principle is important if you want to highlight certain areas of your quilt. The clever placement of light, medium, and dark values can create optical illusions, as seen below.

In your quilts, you will use a variety of prints (patterned fabrics) and solid-color fabrics, also called plains. Use a combination of small-, medium-, and large-scale prints in your work. Remember that small-scale prints will appear, or read, solid from a distance. However, they are often a more interesting choice than a plain solid color.

For piecing and appliqué, use 100 percent cotton fabrics. Cotton handles well and will take a crease; thus, it suits appliqué, and it presses well for piecing. Not all fabrics labeled "100 percent cotton" are the same, and not all are right for quilt making.

Cotton can include knits, corduroy, upholstery fabrics, broderie anglaise, and sailcloth. Fabrics like these, especially knits, are best avoided by beginners although sometimes they suit the inspirations of a more experienced quilter.

Look at the weave of the fabric—a loose-weave fabric allows the batting to escape, and tightly woven fabrics are difficult to hand quilt. Dress-weight cottons are best for beginners. If an upholstery fabric appeals to you but you are unsure about whether you should use it, imagine wearing a blouse made with it. If you think it would be comfortable, then it is probably appropriate for your quilt.

Polyester-cotton blends can be used for piecing, provided they are more than 50 percent cotton. They are not suitable for hand appliqué, as they do not stay turned under long enough to be stitched into place. They are better used as backgrounds for appliqué. Beware when pressing: an iron hot enough to press the cotton pieces may slightly shrink the blended fabrics.

Some techniques require special fabrics. Crazy patchwork uses velvets, brocades, satins, and silks. Sheer organdy is used for shadow appliqué. Silk is a favorite of experienced quilters, although it is not recommended for a beginner's first project.

If you decide to recycle fabrics, make sure that they are not too distressed, or you will find yourself having to repair or replace worn patches after the quilt is finished. Wherever possible, use fabrics of similar weight and type in one project.

**Above:** *Tumbling Blocks* detail, American, early twentieth century.

## Buying Fabric

Fabrics come in a variety of different widths. The most readily available is 44 to 45 inches wide, and most of the fabric requirements listed in our projects are based on this width.

There is a good range of solid colors available in 60-inch-wide fabrics. A few specialty fabrics, such as Liberty's Tana Lawn, are produced only in 36-inch widths.

Muslin is often used for backing quilts, backgrounds of blocks, and home-dyeing. It is available in a range of widths, from 36 to 108 inches. This diversity makes it a more practical choice for backing quilts of any size because you can simply buy the width that best fits the project at hand.

Buying fat quarters (18 inches long x 22 inches wide) is a very convenient way to buy small amounts of many fabrics. The cut is made by dividing a yard of 44- to 45-inch-wide fabric in half both vertically and horizontally. Often, a fat quarter is a more useful shape than the conventional ¼-yard cut (long quarter), which yields a piece 9 inches long x 44–45 inches wide. However, for a project requiring a few long, narrow strips, the latter would be more suitable. Although many quilting stores sell fat quarters, be aware that some sell fabric only in conventional cuts.

## Preparing Fabric

Prewash new fabrics before storing. This should be done immediately after purchase. Washing removes the sizing (making the fabric easier to work with) as well as any excess dye. Sort your fabrics into darks, mediums, and lights. Wash separately in warm water with a tiny amount of mild soap. It is not unusual to notice some traces of color in the water. This color would not normally transfer onto other fabrics when sewn into a quilt. However, if a fabric sheds a lot of dye in the rinse, it is probably not colorfast and further washing is advisable.

Alternatively, soak the fabric for a few hours in a solution of one part salt or vinegar to three parts water. After washing, when the fabric is almost dry, straighten the grain if necessary. Do this by first pulling the fabric diagonally across in both directions and then again in the direction in which it appears short. Bring the selvages together and press very lightly down the length of the fabric. Fold the fabric neatly and allow to dry completely before storing.

## Selvage and Grain

The selvage is the tightly woven edge of the fabric and should be trimmed before cutting.

The grain is the direction of the threads in woven fabric. The lengthwise grain (warp) runs parallel to the selvage and has very little stretch. The crosswise grain (weft) runs at right angles to the selvage and is slightly stretchy. The diagonal direction is the bias. It has the most stretch, making it ideal for bindings. Whenever possible, place the weft and the warp parallel to the outer edges of the block. Always mark the grain lines on templates and pattern pieces.

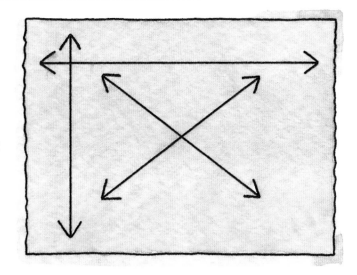

# MAKING AND USING TEMPLATES

Always begin with a full-size draft of the design or block to be sewn. Label each shape with a letter or number and mark with the grain line of the pieces. Have the straight grain of the fabric parallel to the edges of the block. Keep this master draft of the block or design to use as a reference at any stage of the work.

## MATERIALS FOR MAKING TEMPLATES

- Template plastic
  (plastic is more durable and should be chosen if a shape will be used many times over)
- Ruler
- Fine-line permanent marker
- Craft knife or scissors
- Pencil
- Glue stick

## Templates for Hand Piecing

> Templates for hand piecing do not include a seam allowance.

**1** To make a template with template plastic, place the see-through plastic over a full-size draft of the block. Using a fine-line marker, trace one of each shape required. Cut the shapes exactly on the marker line without adding seam allowances.

**2** Check that the templates you have made fit the master draft. If they are inaccurate, the mistake will be compounded as you sew the quilt.

**3** Label the template and add the grain line on the wrong side of the template. For cutting, the template will be placed wrong side up on the wrong side of the fabric.

**4** To make cardboard templates, first make a copy of the draft block, then carefully cut apart the paper copy. Turn over each piece before gluing to cardboard. Cut out the cardboard shapes without adding any seam allowances.

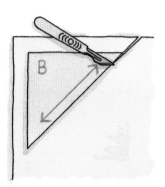

**5** Check that the templates fit your master draft. Label the pieces and transfer the grain line of each to the appropriate template. Many quilters also add the number of times the shape must be cut.

## Templates for Machine Piecing

> Templates for machine piecing include a ¼-inch seam allowance.

**1** Using template plastic, start as for hand-piecing templates; however, add a ¼-inch seam allowance on all sides of your tracing outline. Cut out carefully along the new outline. Check against the master draft and label.

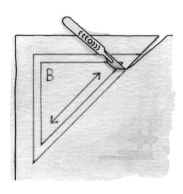

## Templates for Hand Appliqué

To make plastic or cardboard templates for hand appliqué, follow the directions for hand piecing. Do not turn them over before labeling.

In appliqué, the templates are placed on the right side of the fabric ready for marking.

If you are working with light-colored fabrics, trace the shape directly onto the right side of the fabric from the master pattern.

## Quilting Templates

Make quilting templates from durable material, preferably template plastic, as standard designs are likely to be used for several projects. Follow the instructions as for making templates for hand piecing and remember to cut out the interior spaces.

## Window Templates

A window template provides you with a seam line and a cutting line in one template. It is also a useful device for viewing fabric motifs.

Make a template as for machine piecing with accurate ¼-inch seam allowances but do not turn the shape over. Cut out the shape from the center of the template to leave a window with a ¼-inch frame.

## Register or Repeat Templates

Make a plastic register, or repeat, template if you want to put the same part of the fabric pattern in the same position in each block. This is not an economical use of fabric, so you will need more fabric than given in the materials list.

❶ Depending on your working method, whether hand or machine sewing, make a template for the required shape.

❷ Place the template over the fabric print as you want it to appear in the finished block. With a permanent fine-line marker, draw the outline of the motif onto the plastic so that each time you are able to position it correctly before cutting out the fabric.

# CUTTING

There are important differences in the way fabric is cut for hand or machine piecing and hand appliqué. Please read the directions carefully and practice on some spare fabric.

## Preparing for Cutting

**1** If you have not already washed your fabrics, do so before starting a new project. If you suspect any of your fabrics are not colorfast, see page 25 for further instructions.

**2** Straighten the grain of the fabric by first pulling the fabric diagonally across in both directions and then again in the direction in which the fabric appears short. Bring the selvages together and press very lightly down the length of the fabric.

**3** Trim away the selvages. If you do not, they will feel like hard ridges under your work. Selvages are tightly woven to stabilize the fabric and after washing often shrink, causing the fabric to pucker.

**4** Steam-press all fabrics carefully before cutting. After washing, some fabrics become limp. This makes them difficult to cut; a light spray of starch during pressing can improve their behavior.

**5** Work out your cutting order and cut all the pieces for a project at one time. As a rule, cut the larger pieces first and work down to the smallest. Many quilters like to cut odd-shaped pieces from one end of the fabric, keeping the other end intact for cutting long strips.

## Cutting for Hand Piecing

**1** Lay the prepared fabric right side down on a flat surface. Place your templates on the wrong side of the fabric, allowing space for the ¼-inch seam allowances on all sides of the shapes. With a sharp pencil, trace around the shape. On dark fabric use a white or light-colored pencil, or a sharpened sliver of dry soap. Keep the pencil angled well in toward the template edges for accuracy.
　If the fabric is unstable and slides on your work surface, place it on top of a sheet of fine sandpaper before marking.

**2** Cut out the shapes, adding the ¼-inch seam allowance by eye.

## Cutting for Hand Appliqué

**1** Place the prepared fabric on a flat surface, right side up, and carefully draw around the template. Or, if using a light-colored fabric, place over the design and trace off.

**2** Leave enough space between shapes to add by eye a ⅛- to ¼-inch seam allowance on all sides as you cut.

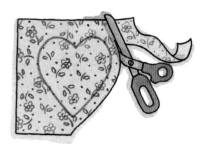

## Cutting for Machine Piecing

**1** Place your templates on the wrong side of the fabric and with a well-sharpened pencil draw carefully around each template. Unlike templates for hand piecing, templates for machine use include seam allowances in the measurements, so you can place templates adjacent to each other.

**2** Cut carefully, and exactly, on the pencil line; if you can still see the pencil line after cutting, the piece will be a fraction too large and this error will be compounded as the work progresses. If you have lost the pencil line, then your piece will be too small.

## Rotary Cutting

The use of rotary cutters in conjunction with plastic rulers and self-healing cutting mats has revolutionized quilt-making. It is a fast and accurate method that allows you to cut through up to eight layers of fabric with a single pass of the blade. Even a beginner working on a single layer of fabric and cutting one piece at a time will find the process easy.

Rotary cutting entails cutting strips and cutting the strips into smaller units, such as squares, rectangles, triangles, and diamonds. As a result of this method of strip-cutting, a number of speed-piecing techniques have developed. (See pages 64–81 in the Patchwork section for further information.)

Rotary cutting saves you time, but you can just as quickly cut up lots of fabric incorrectly, so choose a piece of fabric you are willing to sacrifice for a practice session.

The instructions are given for right-handed quilters. If you are left-handed, you will have to reverse all the instructions.

### TIPS

- The cutter has an exceptionally sharp blade. Never lay it down without engaging the safety guard.
- Always roll the cutter away from yourself.
- Make sure the mat is clear of unwanted objects, such as pins, before spreading out the fabric for cutting. Rolling over a pin will permanently damage the blade.
- Practice presenting the cutter toward the side of the ruler from the side, just above the surface of the mat, rather than with a chopping action from above. This prevents it from catching on the edge or corner of the plastic ruler, which damages both blade and ruler.
- When cutting fabric, take care not to let the cutter run off the edge of the mat; this will damage the blade and the surface beneath.
- Never leave the mat against anything warm, such as a radiator, or in direct sunlight, as it will warp.

# Preparation for Cutting Strips

All fabrics should be prepared in the following way to ensure starting with a truly squared piece of fabric. Even with practice, it is not unusual when cutting large numbers of pieces to find strips beginning to drift, so be prepared to square up the end of the fabric again if necessary. This preparatory precision is essential for accurate results.

**1** Press a piece of fabric that without folding almost fits the mat.

**2** Find one side of the fabric that is true to the grain, such as the selvage, and align it with one of the grid lines printed on the mat.

**3** Trim away the selvage by placing the ruler over the fabric with the right-hand edge of the ruler parallel to the selvage and ¼ inch away from it. Hold the ruler down with your left hand without shifting its position. Place your ring finger against the left-hand edge of the ruler to help keep the ruler in place.

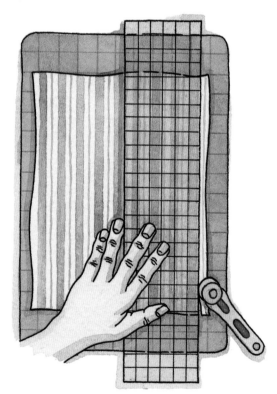

**4** With the cutter in your right hand, flat side toward the ruler, disengage the guard. Start cutting at the edge of the fabric by positioning the cutter to the right of the ruler, almost touching the uncovered mat. Bring the side of the

blade toward the side of the ruler; only when it touches the ruler should you put the blade down on the mat. This avoids damage to both the blade and the ruler. With the cutter at a 45° angle to the mat, roll it away from you across the fabric. Only a slight downward pressure is needed. It takes practice to maintain an even pressure.

Variation in pressure during cutting can result in uncut sections. Slight pressure toward the left keeps the blade against the ruler, but too much pressure can push the ruler out of place.

**5** When you have cut the fabric, close the guard carefully and, without disturbing the fabric, slide the ruler away to the left and remove the trimmings.

**6** To straighten a side adjacent to the trimmed selvage ready for cutting strips, turn the mat 90° and place the right-hand edge of the ruler close to the right-hand side of the fabric. Also align one of the cross lines on the ruler with the trimmed selvage edge. Cut across the fabric away from yourself. You should now have a good straight edge from which to cut additional strips.

**7** To avoid disturbing your now carefully prepared fabric, simply turn the cutting mat around so that the trimmed end is on the left-hand side. Position your ruler on the edge of the fabric at the desired width to cut your strips. Proceed to cut as in step 4.

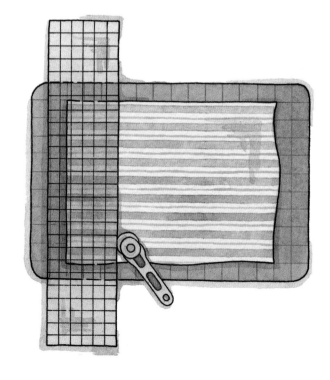

# Cutting a Single Layer of Fabric

**Cutting squares** Carefully position one of your strips against a grid line on the mat to make sure it is straight. Place the ruler over the left-hand end of the strip at the required width. Check that the line is at right angles to the long sides of the strip before cutting off the first square.

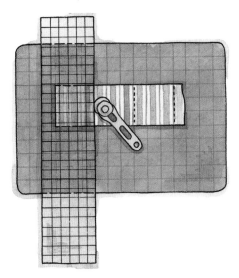

**Cutting half-square triangles** First cut a square (see above), then position it so that two opposite corners align with a grid line on the mat. Place your ruler along the same line and carefully cut the square diagonally into two right-angle triangles.

To estimate the size of square needed to cut a half-square triangle with the necessary ¼-inch seam allowances on all three sides, add ⅞ inch to each of the two short sides of the triangle.

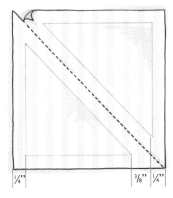

**Cutting quarter-square triangles** These are made by cutting a square across both diagonals.

To estimate the size of square needed to cut a quarter-square triangle, add 1¼ inches to the long side of the full-size triangle.

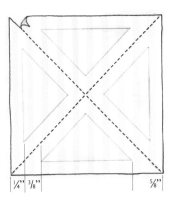

**Cutting diamonds** To estimate the width of strip needed for cutting diamonds, draw a ¼-inch outline around your pattern and measure the distance between the parallel lines. This distance will be the width of strip you need to cut.

Make a paper template of the diamond and attach it to the underside of your plastic ruler. Use it as a marker for cutting.

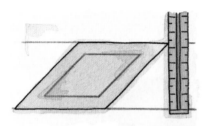

## Cutting Several Layers of Fabric

A small cutter with a sharp blade can cut up to six layers of fabric; a large cutter can cut up to eight.

❶ Press the fabrics to remove any creases.

❷ When cutting just two separate pieces of fabric, place one over the other and press so that they "cling" together.

❸ If you are cutting a large piece of fabric, you will need to fold it several times to fit the mat. When there is only a single fold,

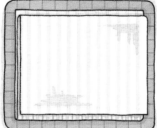

place the fold to face you. If the fabric is too wide to be folded only once, fold it accordion-style to fit your mat. To ensure that your cut strips are straight and even, the folds must be placed exactly parallel to the straight edges of the fabric and you must cut at right angles to both the cut edges and the folds.

❹ To cut, follow step 4 in Preparation for Cutting Strips on page 30. The more layers you cut, the greater the downward pressure you need to apply to the blade. The pressure must remain constant, or variations will result and the lower layers of fabric may not be fully cut.

❺ Rotary-cut pieces are generally machine-sewn, but if you prefer to hand sew, mark your sewing line with a pencil dot at the corners of your pieces ¼ inch from both edges.

## Storing Cut Pieces

• Stack all the cut pieces together in like groups.

• Label the pieces, perhaps with a strip of paper wrapped around them, and place in a plastic storage bag; alternatively, thread all the pieces on a length of sewing cotton.

• Store the pieces flat, taking care not to fray or stretch the edges by overhandling the shapes.

## Cutting Irregular Shapes

For more unusual shapes, a template also will be needed. Place the template on the strip and mark and cut in the traditional way.

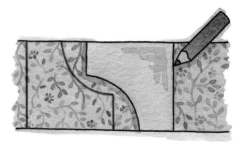

# HAND PIECING AND MACHINE PIECING

The pieces for the blocks can be sewn together either by hand or by machine. Instructions are given for both methods, and it is acceptable to mix hand and machine work in a quilt top. The advantage of machine sewing over hand sewing is twofold: speed and strength. However, hand stitchers will vigorously argue that it is easier to match seams, sew curves, and inset by hand. Handwork is also portable; it can be picked up at any time and any place.

## Hand Piecing

**1** Work a trial block to decide on the sewing order. Mark the pieces on the wrong side with a pencil outline of the finished shape.

**2** Place two pieces together with right sides facing. Insert a pin straight through (like a spear) from the corner of one piece to the matching corner of the other. Repeat at other end. Insert more pins across the sewing line.

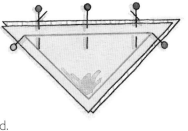

**3** Thread a sharps needle with about 15 inches of matching thread. Knot at one end and remove the "spear" pin at one corner. Insert your needle on the pencil line ⅙ inch in from the corner and make a small backstitch.

**4** Sew small, even running stitches along the pencil line from one marked corner to the other. Try not to stretch the fabric as you go. Turn your sewing over sometimes to check that the stitches are on the pencil line on both sides.

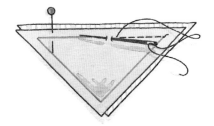

**5** To avoid a weak spot at the end, turn and sew back two stitches, and then make a couple of stitches on the spot.

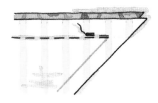

**6** Press the sewn pieces as directed in the Pressing section on page 36.

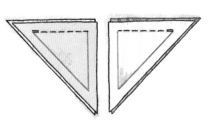

**7** When sewing together pieced units, do not stitch across the seam allowance at the seam junctions. This will allow you to press the seams in any direction.

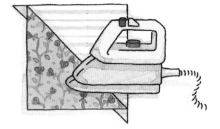

**8** Precisely matching the marked corners, pass your needle through the seam allowance to the other side and proceed to sew.

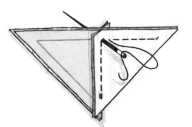

## Machine Piecing

The sewing lines are not marked for machine piecing; instead, the edges of the pieces are used as a guide for sewing. Therefore, to get the best results when piecing by machine, first check that you can achieve a ¼-inch seam allowance consistent with your seam allowances established for cutting (see opposite).

## Sewing

In machine piecing, the stitching extends into the seam allowances. This means that pressing as you sew is essential. You must decide how you want to press the seams at each step before you proceed to the next stage.

❶ Pin two pieces right sides together with the pins at right angles to the line of sewing. Prepare several units at one time.

❷ Place the pairs under the presser foot, right-hand edges against the guide, and, holding the thread tails to one side, start to sew. As the pieces pass through the machine, keep their edges level with the guide and let them feed through with as little steering as possible. Do not pull them through, as this will stretch the seam, especially on bias edges.

❸ Chain sewing saves time and thread when you are sewing multiple units. At the end of the seam, stop sewing just beyond the edge of the fabric and leave the sewn pair in place while you feed in the next pair. The seams will not come apart provided there are a couple of stitches between each unit. Press the seams of each unit. They can be pressed while joined, then cut apart.

❹ When sewing pieced units together, match the internal seam and ease as necessary. The block will look better if intersecting seams match, even if this means that the raw edges do not finish level.

**Above:** *Mariner's Compass* block, American, nineteenth century.

**Above:** *Flying Dutchman* block, American, nineteenth century.

# Checking the Seam Allowance

**1** The sewing machine may be supplied with either a ¼-inch foot, or with a throat plate marked in ⅛-inch gradations. In this case, simply check that these match your seam allowances used for cutting by sliding the ruler under the machine foot at right angles to you, with the ¼-inch mark directly below the machine needle. To make this easier, rotate the balance wheel by hand to bring the needle close to the ruler. When correctly aligned, lower the presser foot to hold the ruler in place and check by both looking and feeling whether the edge of the ruler and the presser foot are level or whether the edge of the ruler matches the mark on the throat plate. If so, these markings may be followed to guide your piecing.

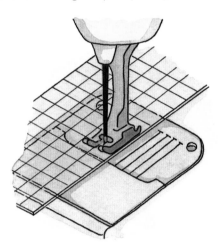

**2** Alternatively, position the ruler as in step 1 and place a strip of masking tape right against the edge of the ruler to use as a guideline. After positioning the tape, you may need to cut a slit in the tape to allow the throat plate to be opened.

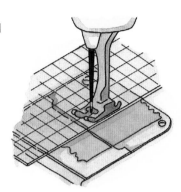

**3** If you are cutting using templates, check the seam allowances in a similar way. On paper mark two lines ¼ inch apart, ruled with the same measure used to add the seam allowances to the templates. Place the paper under the machine with the needle unthreaded and the right-hand line against the edge of the presser foot. Sew along the paper a little, then look to see whether the stitching is along the left-hand line. If not, some machines allow the needle to be repositioned slightly to bring it to the required point to sew along the drawn line.

Alternatively, trim the paper to the right-hand line. Place test paper under the presser foot with the needle into the left-hand line. Lower the presser foot and add a strip of masking tape against the paper as your sewing guide.

---

# Easing Seams

Sometimes, blocks that must be sewn together do not come up to the same size. In this case, they must be eased between the matched seams.

To do this, have the longer of the two blocks facing you. With your thumbs, spread the fullness away from the center toward the matched seams (fig. 1), and place a pin in the middle (fig. 2).

**fig. 3**                    **fig. 4**

Repeat this to spread the fullness equally in first half (fig. 3), and then the other half of the blocks (fig. 4). If necessary, repeat again in each of the four quarters.

Often, the action of the sewing machine helps the easing process if the "long" side is below and the "short" side is on top. This is because the machine tends to stretch the top layer of fabric when two layers are sewn together.

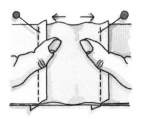 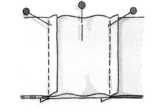

**fig. 1**                    **fig. 2**

# PRESSING

To do justice to your sewing, it is important to press your work carefully. Pressing for sewing is not the same as doing household ironing. To press, lift the iron and set it down on, rather than sliding it across, the fabric.

Whether you choose to use a steam or dry iron is chiefly a matter of personal preference. When using steam, take extra care not to distort the fabric. If you have a dry iron, a light mister will be useful for stubborn creases. To prevent fabrics from glazing, use a pressing cloth when pressing the right side of fabrics. Press with the grain line—do not stretch bias edges.

## Pressing Seams

It is always good advice to sew a test block before beginning a major project. This will allow you to try different ways of pressing it to see which looks best. Sometimes, the same block will be pressed differently according to how it will be quilted.

- Press the seam allowance in the closed position first, then in the direction you want.

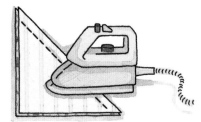

- Press the seam allowances to one side, not open as for dressmaking. This holds the seams more securely and prevents the wadding from "seeping" through the seam.

- Wherever possible, press toward the darker fabrics. If this is not possible, reduce the dark shadow that will appear through the light fabric by trimming the dark seam allowance slightly narrower than the light.

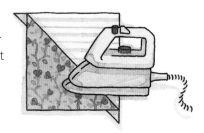

- If you have decided on your quilting plan, press the seam allowances away from the areas you wish to quilt. It is very difficult to quilt over the hard edges of seams.

- Always press seams before sewing across them in another direction.

- When joining fabric for additional length, press the seam open, as it will have less effect on the quilting design that may cross it. The same applies to strips joined for binding. Seams pressed open will cause less of a ridge.

- Sometimes a complex intersection of seams may not look accurate; rather than unpicking the block and resewing, try pressing the seam allowances in a different direction. It is surprising how much improvement this can make. If you need to unpick a seam, first press the pieces closed again (right sides together). This makes it easier to get the seam unpicked into the threads with less chance of damaging the cloth.

- When a block has a multiple-seam joint, press all the seam allowances in the same direction, rotating around the block, regardless of the color of the individual pieces. This will help reduce the bulk. Often, the piecing sequence for

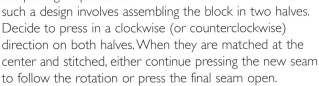

such a design involves assembling the block in two halves. Decide to press in a clockwise (or counterclockwise) direction on both halves. When they are matched at the center and stitched, either continue pressing the new seam to follow the rotation or press the final seam open.

- Using a checkered fabric or a specially designed quilter's cover marked with a grid over your ironing board makes it easy to see whether a block is the correct size and shape.

# Finger-pressing

Finger-pressing is fast but not a permanent way of pressing small areas of fabric. Position the seam allowance, then press down on the seam. Move your fingers to a new position and press down again; continue until the entire seam has been treated. Take care not to stretch the seam by running your fingers and pulling along the seam.

## Pressing for Appliqué

1 For a smooth finish, press your appliqué shapes before turning the raw edges under.

2 To avoid flattening the sewn shapes, place a towel on the ironing board and cover this with a dish towel or pressing cloth. Place the work right side down and press gently.

## Pressing for Quilt Assembly

Deciding how to press seam allowances when assembling the blocks, sashings, and borders is often a matter of common sense. The quilting plan may influence some decisions. For instance, if you plan to quilt in-the-ditch, the seams should be pressed in the same way for every repeat in order to achieve a consistent appearance.

● After sewing blocks together in rows, press all the seams of odd-numbered rows in one direction and in the opposite direction for even-numbered rows. As the rows of blocks are stitched, the alternate pressing directions will lock the rows together, making your work more accurate.

● When pieced blocks are sewn to unpieced alternate squares, press the seams toward the unpieced blocks. This also forms locking intersections when rows of blocks are joined.

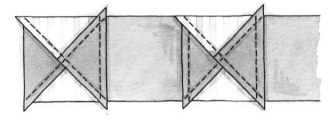

● Appliqué quilts in which blocks are set side by side may have their seams pressed open. Quilted all around the appliqué motifs, the pressed-open seams will barely be noticeable.

● After assembling rows, press seams toward the top of the quilt. With multiple borders, press each before sewing. Press open seams in sashing or framing strips to make them less noticeable and press seam allowances of framing or border strips away from the center toward the edges of the block or quilt.

● Give the assembled quilt top a final thorough but gentle press before layering with the backing and batting.

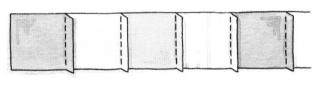

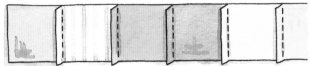

# SETTING AND FRAMING

Ask six quilters to sew the same pieced blocks into a quilt, and each, by choosing a different setting and framing, will come up with a different design for the top.

Setting refers to the way in which the various parts of the quilt top are arranged. There are innumerable ways in which the blocks can be put together, and each arrangement creates a different appearance. Blocks set side by side frequently create a striking secondary pattern. Pieced blocks alternated with plain blocks are an effective way of increasing the quilt size without a lot of extra work and offer a good opportunity for elaborate quilting

that would otherwise be lost among the seams of a pieced block.

Framing describes the sewing of pieces of fabric around a block or group of blocks. Framing is a useful device, as it can unify blocks of different pattern, color, or size.

Using the simple two-colored Underground Railroad block, the examples below give some indication of the variety of sets possible.

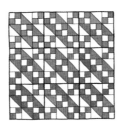

**1** Single Underground Railroad block.

**2** Straight blocks set side by side with the same orientation.

**3** Straight blocks set side by side with alternating orientation.

**4** Straight blocks with alternating coloring and orientation, and mitered framing.

**5** Framed straight blocks with alternating coloring and orientation using sashing squares.

**6** Straight set blocks, alternating color and orientation with vertical sashing only.

**7** Blocks set on-point, side by side with the same orientation.

**8** Blocks set on-point with alternating colored sashing squares.

**9** Blocks set on-point with alternating colored sashing squares and corner triangles.

# BORDERS

There is never a time when the border of a quilt doesn't matter. Even if you make miniatures, the border may still occupy between 20–25 percent of the area. An effective border can transform a mediocre center into an attractive quilt and lift a strong and interesting center into excellence.

Having said that, having no border can be a deliberate choice. The Log Cabin quilt, page 92, the Pineapple variation, page 96 and the Colorwash with White Triangles, page 116 all work well visually with the design running to the quilt edges.

The border can function as a frame, e.g., the Vase of Flowers wall hanging, page 118. Like a picture frame, it separates the center from surroundings over which you have no control, so can be advisable for wall hangings.

Displaying the center to best advantage is also a reason for thinking of the border as a visual rest area. While not an excuse for doing nothing, this means that the border should not compete with the center for the viewer's attention, such as by introducing entirely new elements. A simple sequence of two or three strips, carefully color coordinated (as with the Vase of Flowers), or a simplified element from the center might be wise solutions.

The border should look as if it belongs just to this quilt rather than a catchall for every quilt you make. The most usual way to achieve this integration is by visually repeating the center in some way. This could be reusing fabrics from the center, picking up colors or repeating motifs, perhaps in simplified form. The Double Nine-patch, page 67, has a border of squares on point which echo the nine-patch blocks from the center while being simpler as they are not pieced. A reinterpretation of a motif from the center can work well, as seen in the decorative appliqué border of the Baltimore Basket quilt, page 140. Though the bows in the border are different in form from those in the center, they sit happily together. We accept them as related, and their strong simplicity complements the detail of the center well.

Finally, the border does not have to be the same on all sides, though new quilters often imagine this to be so. Vary the width and content as you please to suit your project. Examples include the Flying Geese quilt, page 74, which only has borders on the two shortest sides.

## Planning Your Border

- Measure across the center of the quilt, vertically and horizontally, to find the required border lengths. Cut borders for your project a little oversized as insurance.

- Planning is more about thinking than drawing. Ask yourself questions about one aspect of the border at a time. Write down your answers to form a list of how you'd like the border to look. Next think about how to achieve this, again recording your ideas.

- Studying the list, decide from the options you have listed which ones you think will work best. Consider the future home of the quilt if you know it to help guide your decision. Your solution may incorporate several, though rarely all, of the ideas collected above.

- Finally, never settle for the first idea you have—better ones almost always appear! If you note the first idea, it will still be there for you to choose if it promises to be the best.

**Above:** Medallion style quilt, by Sally Connor, British, late twentieth century.

**Page 38:** *Underground Railroad*, American, ca. 1870. In this mid-nineteenth century quilt, the secondary crisscross diamond pattern is created by alternating the color and orientation of the blocks.

**Left:** *Joseph's Coat*, American, Mennonite, ca. 1920.

# Mitered Borders

Making the required 45° angle at the corner for the miter uses more fabric and requires careful handling of the bias seams.

❶ Decide on the border width. Double this figure and add to all length measurements for cutting the borders. To add a 7-inch border to a 36 × 48-inch quilt top, cut two strips 50 × 6 inches and two strips 62 × 6 inches.

❷ As in step 2 for straight-cut borders, divide the quilt and border edges and pin borders to opposite sides of the quilt top.

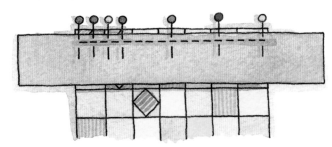

❸ Start sewing the first border ¼ inch from the corner, using a ¼-inch seam allowance, and stop ¼ inch from the end. Fold borders already attached out of the way and repeat to add the remaining borders.

❹ To find where to sew the miter seam, with the quilt wrong side up, fold both border ends at each corner as follows:

**(a)** Finger-press a continuation of the ¼-inch seam that attaches the border and pin temporarily.

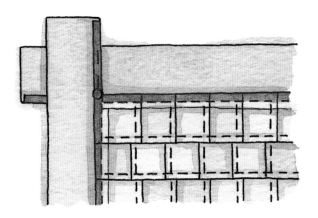

**(b)** Fold the end back along the border so the pinned turning is level with the existing seam. This makes a fold at right angles to the first seam, in line with the other seam coming to the corner. Lightly finger-press this fold.

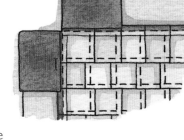

**(c)** Grasp the end of the border and bring it out to the side of the quilt to align the pinned turning with the fold just made in step b. This makes a 45° angled fold at the end of the border. Finger-press without stretching. Repeat for the other border strip.

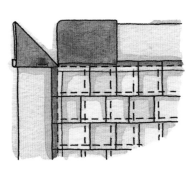

❺ Fold the quilt top right sides together diagonally through the corner so that the two miter folds are on top of each other. Pin across the fold. Before sewing, check that they lie together neatly without any little tucks at the inner corner.

❻ Sew by hand or by machine. If machine sewing, set the stitch length to 0 and insert the needle right where the previous stitching ended. Sew a stitch or two before changing to normal length to sew the seam outward toward the corner. Keep the work well supported to avoid stretching the seam as you sew.

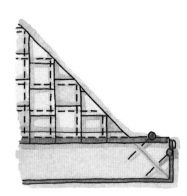

❼ Check that the miter is neat and true before pressing the seam open and trimming any excess fabric. Work all four corners in the same way.

## Straight-cut Borders

**1** Determine your border width. Cut two strips the border width x the length of the quilt side. Cut two strips the border width x the length of the quilt width, plus twice the border width. For example, for a 36 x 50-inch quilt with 6-inch borders, cut two side borders, each 6 x 50 inches; for the top and bottom borders, cut strips 6 x 48 inches.

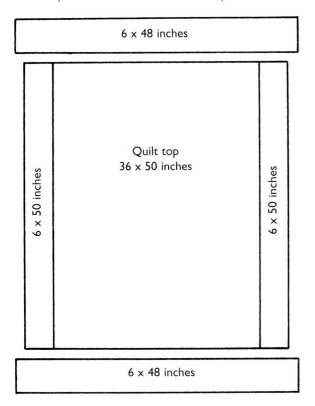

**2** Divide the quilt side and the side borders into halves and quarters. With right sides facing and raw edges level, match these points and pin across the seam line. Continue pinning, easing the top onto the border, then sew carefully.

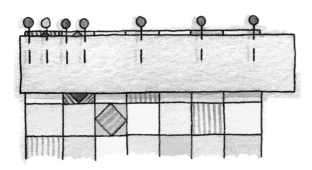

**3** Check the appearance before pressing. Trim any excess, ensuring that the corner of the quilt is square. Repeat to add the opposite border.

**4** Add top and bottom borders and check before pressing. The borders should lie flat when the quilt lies on a flat surface. Trim any excess.

## Multiple Mitered Borders

If you want multiple borders around the quilt, sew strips of the required fabrics into sets and attach these to the sides of the quilt top. This allows you still to sew only one miter at each corner, matching up the colors, instead of struggling to sew separate miters for each round of color.

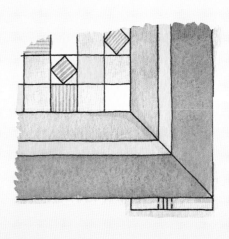

## Fancy Borders

In this category are designs featuring pieced borders, scalloped edges, and appliqué borders. What they have in common is the anxiety they cause about fitting the chosen pattern into a given space. The rule-of-thumb method below, although written for a scalloped edge, will work just as well for dividing up and planning the swags or stems of an appliqué border.

### Devising a Scalloped Border

Practice the process in miniature on a small strip of paper. For a rectangular quilt, some initial calculation is required to find a number that divides evenly into both sides so that scallops of the same size appear all around the quilt. To make the calculations easier, you may need to adjust the overall size of the quilt.

**1** Decide how many scallops you want on the side of the quilt. Cut a strip of paper as long as the side of the quilt. Fold the strip in half.

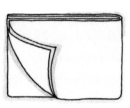 

**2** Fold in half again. Mark the number of scallop divisions with an accordion-style fold. Unfold half.

**3** Using the edge of a plate as a template, mark the curve between the two fold lines. When choosing the plate size,

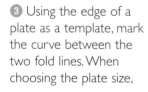 

consider the design of the quilt. It may already have a curved design that you want to echo. Remember that gentle curves will be much easier to sew.

**4** Refold the paper but keep the marked scallop where you can see it on the outside. When all the folds are back in place correctly, you should have half of the marked scallop visible as a guide for cutting the curve. If the layers of paper will permit, staple them together before cutting for a more accurate result. Cut along the curve and unfold.

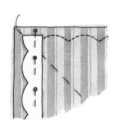

**5** Lay the paper pattern on the quilt top and check that the curves are smooth and the correct size. When satisfied, pin the paper pattern to the quilt and mark the outline with basting stitches.

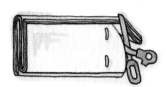

**6** Baste lines at a 45° angle in the corners to help fit the pattern. The outline of the pattern will be the edge of the quilt. This shows you how far to take your quilting design. Do not cut the scallops until you are ready to bind the edges of the quilt top.

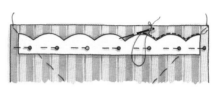

**7** Bind with a single narrow 1-inch bias binding.

---

### TIPS FOR BACKINGS

- Choose fabrics that are easy to quilt.
- Beginners are advised to choose small prints to disguise irregularities in quilting.
- Do not choose dark backings, which may show through light-colored tops.
- The color of the quilting thread may influence color choice for backing.
- Ensure the backing will be larger than the top.
- Wash and iron backing fabric before use.
- When joining fabric widths, avoid having backing seams coinciding with major seams on the quilt top.
- To avoid a center seam when two widths are needed to make up the backing, divide one piece equally in two and sew one to each side of the center piece.
- If joining selvages, make ½ to ¾-inch seams (depending on the actual appearance of the selvage), then trim away the hard edge before pressing the seam open for less bulk.
- Backings can include spare blocks from the front or be assembled from several different pieces of fabric that may continue the theme of the quilt.
- Labels can be pieced into the backing—it is then impossible for anyone to remove them.
- The backing can even be a complete design in its own right, making the quilt two sided.

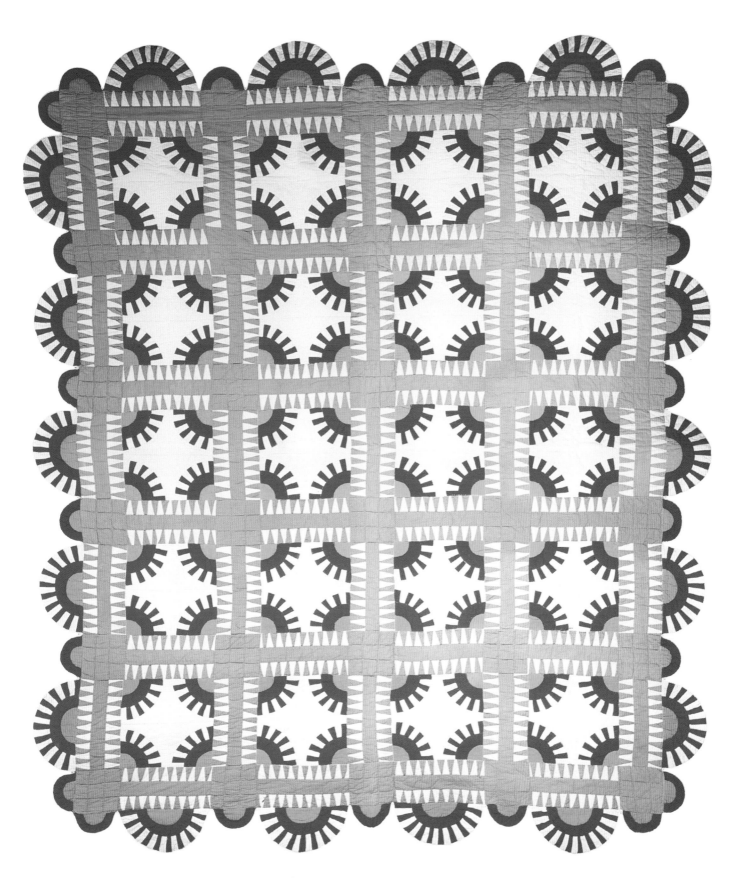

**Above:** *New York Beauty*, American, 1920s or 1930s.

# ASSEMBLING THE QUILT

The quilt top is made by sewing the individual blocks into rows and then joining the rows together horizontally. The quilt pattern depends on sewing the correct blocks in the correct sequence, and also having them the right way up. Try to be methodical and always check your sequence before sewing.

## Joining Blocks

❶ Press all the blocks and check their size. Each must measure ½ inch larger than its required finished size. This allows for the ¼-inch seam allowance on all sides needed for assembly. Any blocks that are wrong should be either resewn or discarded. If your blocks vary significantly in size, check the following:

- different-weight fabrics used
- grain line on individual pieces may not be consistent between blocks
- pieces not cut precisely
- incorrect seam allowances used
- blocks were made over a long period and your accuracy has improved
- seams pressed incorrectly

❷ Arrange the blocks in their correct positions on a flat surface. Many designs, especially scrap quilts, allow you a great deal of freedom in the placement of your blocks, so keep moving the blocks around until you are happy with the arrangement. If the quilt is intended for a bed, be sure to correctly position the blocks to be the right way when it is on the bed, i.e., with the head at the top.

❸ Starting at the top-left-hand corner of the first row, turn block 2 over block 1 with right sides facing. The block edges should be level on all sides. Making a ¼-inch seam, sew the right-hand edges of the two blocks together, starting at the top edge (fig. 1). Continue sewing pairs together until all the blocks for row 1 are used. (In some designs, there will be an odd block at the end of the row.) If you are machine sewing, the pairs of blocks can be "chain-stitched" (see page 34).

| fig. 1 | fig. 2 |

❹ Sew the pairs of blocks together (fig. 2) until you have completed the top row. Repeat the process to sew the remaining rows of the quilt. Press as directed on page 37.

## Joining Rows

❶ On a flat surface, lay out all the rows in order. Turn row 1 over row 2 with right sides together. Match the seams at each intersection with a pin inserted like a spear through the seams ¼ inch from the edge.

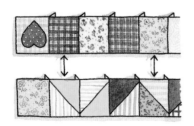

❷ Insert pins at right angles across the sewing line and sew, removing the "spears" before stitching.

**❸** After sewing the two rows together, inspect the seam before pressing, as directed on page 37. Sew all the rows together in pairs, then the pairs together, until the whole top is completely assembled. If your design includes borders, this is the time to sew them on. (For detailed instructions on sewing and applying borders, see pages 42–43.)

**❹** If you choose a quilting design that requires the pattern to be transferred to the top, then it should be done at this stage of assembling the quilt. (Refer to the Quilting section on page 156 for instructions.)

## Layering the Quilt

Making the "quilt sandwich" must be done on a flat surface large enough to accommodate the whole quilt. For large projects, you may find another pair of hands helpful.

**❶** A day or two before you layer the quilt, spread the batting flat to encourage any creases to fall out.

**❷** Press the quilt top thoroughly. Once it is layered, you will not be able to remedy any pressing flaws later.

**❸** Measure the quilt top across the middle, vertically and horizontally. The backing fabric should be about 2 inches larger on all sides to accommodate take-up during quilting. If the backing is not big enough, either replace it with another piece or add an extra strip as necessary.

**❹** Press, then spread the backing right side down, smoothing out any wrinkles. Secure it to the work surface with masking tape.

**❺** Cut the batting marginally smaller than the backing.

**❻** Center the batting over the backing and smooth out carefully without stretching it. If you do not position it correctly at first, lift it up and reposition it; do not drag it into place across the backing. If you are working alone with a piece larger than you can easily handle, try folding it lightly in quarters, then start at the center and unfold carefully.

**❼** Center the quilt top right side up over the batting. Again, do not drag it to adjust its position. There should be an equal amount of batting and backing around all sides of the quilt top (fig. 1).

**❽** Secure the three layers by pinning and then thread-basting, or by pin-basting with safety pins. Start in the center of the quilt and pin the layers together, working out vertically and horizontally, dividing the quilt into quarters. Fill each quarter in a gridlike manner, placing the pins in rows no more than 6 inches apart. Release the backing as

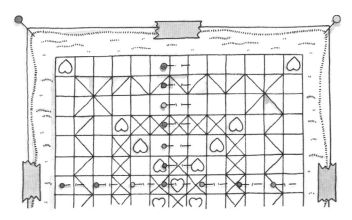

**fig. 1**

it becomes necessary. When the "sandwich" is secure, thread-baste, starting at the center and following the lines of pins. Begin each line of thread with a large knot. The pins can be removed a section at a time (fig. 2). If basting with safety pins, remember that a large number are required for even a modest-size quilt. However, with safety pins there is no need for additional thread-basting.

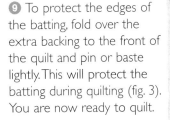

**fig. 2**

**❾** To protect the edges of the batting, fold over the extra backing to the front of the quilt and pin or baste lightly. This will protect the batting during quilting (fig. 3). You are now ready to quilt.

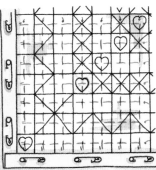

**fig. 3**

# BINDING

Finishing the edges of a quilt is your last chance to refine the design. Self-binding is easy, but the top or the backing must be ¾–1 inch larger than the finished quilt for this method. If the backing is folded to the front, it must suit the design. Separate binding requires more time to complete, but it is versatile. Double binding uses the most fabric, but its firm finish is popular, and the folded edge is easier to sew.

## Fold-finishing

This is a traditional and economical binding method because no extra fabric is needed.

**1** Trim the quilt top to the required size plus the turning, the batting to the finished size, and the backing to the required size plus ½-inch turning.

**2** Fold both turnings to the inside, enclosing the batting with the wider one on the backing.

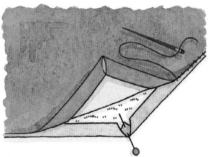

**3** Slipstitch the edges together by hand, or sew through all layers with a running stitch to match the quilting. Alternatively, machine sew.

**4** With a scalloped edge prepare as follows to make them easier to sew. Cut a card template of the curve. Apply a little spray starch with a cotton swab to the turning and with the point of the iron, press the turning over the template. Treat each curve on both the top and backing this way. An alternative is to insert a gathering thread by hand or machine, within the turning, then gather up gently to snug the turning over the template and press.

**5** To insert prairie points, prepare the top edge as in steps 1 and 2. Trim the backing as above and mark the stitching line for attaching the points. Make the prairie points, then baste to the backing, having the points toward the quilt center and the straight edges parallel to the backing edge. Check that they are correctly positioned by making a test fold of the backing over the batting. When correct, baste, then sew the prairie points to the backing. Fold the backing turning to enclose the batting and to flip the points outward. Bring the prepared edge of the top to cover the backing edges and conceal the stitching line, baste in place, then sew.

## Self-binding

**1** Trim the top and batting to the required finished size. Trim the backing as necessary, including a ¾- to 1-inch turning. When ¼ inch is turned in, the former finishes to a ½-inch width, the latter to a ¾-inch width.

**2** Fold the backing to the front, turning in ¼ inch, and pin. Make miters at the corners and baste (fig. 1).

**3** Blind-hem in place (fig. 2) or machine topstitch. If hand sewing add a line or two of quilting next to the hemmed edge to keep the batting from shifting.

**4** To turn the quilt top to the back, reverse the directions.

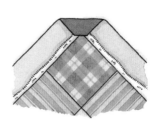

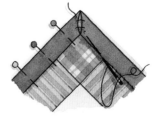

| | |
|---|---|
| **fig. 1** | **fig. 2** |

# Prairie Points

Make singly to use as a decorative feature in a seam. For edging a whole quilt, try the continuous method, which spaces the points evenly.

**1** Fold a square in half right side out. Have the fold at the top. Lightly crease the center vertical.

**2** Fold the top-left and top-right corners down to meet at the center. Crease the diagonals.

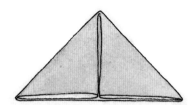

# Continuous Prairie Points

**1** Determine the size of the finished point and, from that, work out the size of the square needed. Cut a fabric strip twice this width and as long as possible. Fold lengthwise, right sides together. Press and fold open.

**2** Divide one half into squares by making a series of cuts as far as the center fold.

**3** On the opposite side, make similar cuts as far as the center fold, halfway between the ones on the first side.

**4** With the strip right side down with one long edge to the top, fold each square in turn down to the center crease, making a fold on the top edge. Then fold the top corners down as for making single prairie points.

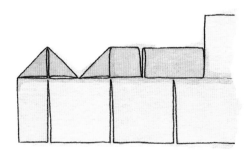

**5** When one side is folded, turn and repeat along the second side.

**6** Refold the fabric lengthwise to make the continuous points.

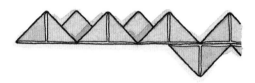

**7** Sew the continuous points into a seam or insert around the edges of a quilt. Used in this way, the quilt edges need to be fold-finished.

**Right:** *Sunflowers* with prairie points binding, American, nineteenth century.

# Single Binding with Automatic Miters

**1** Before binding, prepare the edges of the quilt by trimming the top so that all edges are straight and even. Using a matching thread, machine or hand stitch a row of running stitches through all the layers within the seam allowance. This will hold the layers securely together and help the binding process. The basting stitches will remain permanently in the quilt. If the binding needs replacing, this task will be easier if the layers are fixed.

**2** For a $\frac{1}{4}$-inch finished binding, cut enough strips $1\frac{1}{8}$ inches wide to equal the perimeter of the quilt plus 6–8 inches, when joined.

**3** Beginning along one side of the quilt, but not at the corner, place the raw edge of the binding level with the prepared quilt top. Fold over the end as shown and pin the binding to the quilt as far as the first corner.

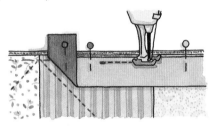

**4** Begin stitching 6 inches from the start of the binding. Check that the basting stitches are covered by the binding.

**5** Stop sewing the width of a seam allowance from the first corner and backstitch a little. Remove your work from the machine.

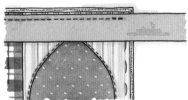

**6** Fold the binding up at a 45° angle, then bring it down parallel with the next side to be sewn and level with the raw edges.

**7** Pin the binding as far as the next corner, then sew.

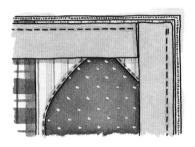

**8** Repeat step 6 at each corner. As you approach the beginning of the binding, stop stitching approximately 6 inches away. Backstitch, then remove the work from the machine.

**9** For a neat diagonal joint without any overlap ridges, fold the tail of the binding over at right angles to itself and match up with the start of the binding, but in the opposite direction. Where the two folds meet is your seam line.

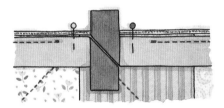

**10** Fold the quilt away from behind the binding, then, with right sides together, machine or hand sew the short diagonal seam.

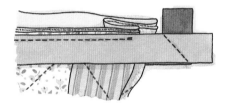

**11** Check that the binding fits accurately all the way around the quilt. Make sure there are no puckers before trimming the excess binding. Finger-press the seam open.

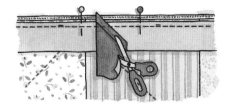

⑫ With the raw edges of the quilt and binding level, sew the remaining short length of pinned binding to the quilt top. Keep your seam allowance consistent to ensure that the two lines of stitching meet in a straight line. Reinforce the joint by backstitching at each end.

⑬ Fold the binding to the back of the quilt. The fullness of the binding at each corner should automatically create neat miters on the quilt front.

⑭ On the back of the quilt, fold in the raw edges of the binding and pin in place. Sew to the machine stitching. Slipstitch the mitered folds as you come to them.

**Above:** *Blazing Star* with two-colored binding, American, nineteenth century.

## Double Binding

**1** Determine the required finished width of your binding and multiply by six: for example, ¼ inch x 6 = 1½ inches. If working with thick fabrics, such as flannels, add another ⅛–¼ inches to accommodate the extra thickness. This is the width of strip to cut either on the straight grain or on the bias.

**2** Fold the binding in half right side out, and press lightly.

**3** As directed for single binding, trim the quilt edges, including the required seam allowance, position the binding with its raw edges to the edge of the quilt, and sew.

**4** Fold the binding to the back of the quilt where the folded edge will be ready to blind-hem to the existing line of stitching.

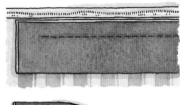

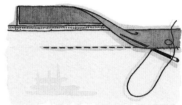

## Continuous Bias

**1** With a rectangle of fabric, right side down (corners must be 90° angles), fold one corner so that the vertical end lines up with the bottom. Press without distorting and cut off the triangle. Repeat at the other end, folding the corner up to the top edge.

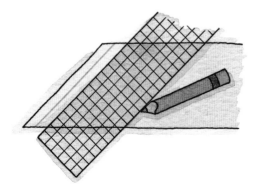

**2** On the wrong side of fabric, draw parallel lines the width of the binding required, measuring at right angles from the first diagonal (shown below). Rule ¼-inch seam lines parallel to the top and bottom edges.

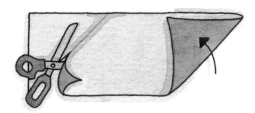

**3** Matching point A to point B with a pin inserted through, fold the fabric right sides together. There is a step at the beginning of the seam. Match each line on the top edge with the appropriate one on the bottom edge.

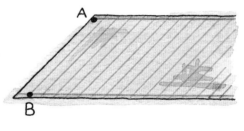

**4** Sew along the marked seam with a short stitch length (15–20 per inch). Check that the ruled lines still match before pressing the seam open.

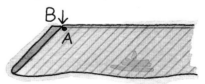

**5** Start at point A–B and cut carefully along the ruled lines around the spiral.

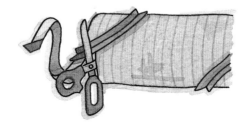

**Above:** *Love and Luck*, American, ca. 1900.

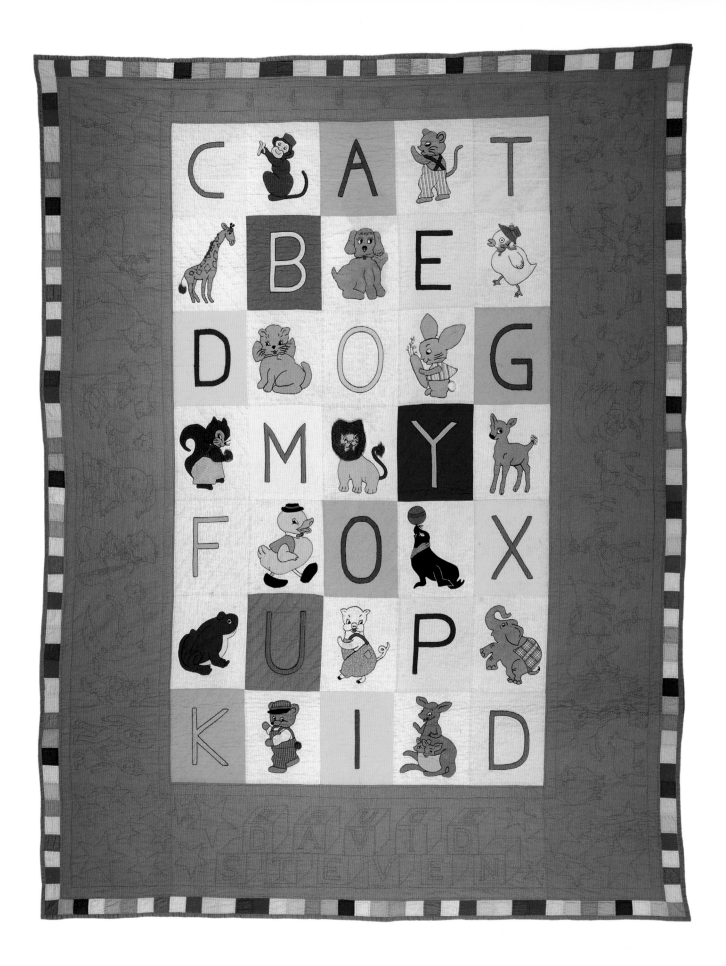

# LABELING AND HANGING

When looking at an old quilt people often wonder who made it, when, and why. This shows us how important it is to label the quilts we make. It is not boastful to label one's work and it may help ensure the quilt's survival in the future.

## Ways to Label

- Labels can be written using a variety of markers designed to be permanent when written on fabric. Written labels are probably the easiest method for adding large amounts of information.
- Labels can be worked using hand or machine embroidery. The time this takes and the scale of line possible may limit how much information you include. Some computerized sewing machines can be programmed to write—useful for labels. An alternative is to set the machine for free embroidery and work directly onto fabric in an embroidery ring.
- Cross-stitch labels are worked through a scrap of canvas waste basted to the label fabric. Plan on graph paper then work carefully without piercing the canvas threads. Soak in water to loosen the glue on the canvas. Allow to partly dry then pull out the canvas threads with tweezers.
- Labels can be decorated with stenciled, printed, or stamped designs as long as the dye, ink, or paint can be fixed.

- A label can be made from an extra pieced block or adorned with appliqué motifs as used on the front.
- If you wish to keep related materials, such as documents, with the quilt, make the label as a pocket or fabric envelope, sewn to the back of the quilt. Seal documents in plastic bags in case they aren't removed before the quilt is washed!

### TIPS FOR LABELS

- The minimum information to include is your name, the date the quilt was finished, and where you live.
- Most quilters enjoy naming their work so include this title. If it is inspired by a quotation, a piece of poetry, or an event, note this too.
- If the quilt is a gift, say who it was for and whether it was for a special occasion. With the possibility of transferring photographs to fabric, you can even add a picture of the owner to the label.

**Above and Right:** Two unique examples of labeling.
**Left:** Alphabet quilt, American, ca.1930. In this quilt the label appears as part of the quilting in the border.

## Preparation of Written Labels

**1** Decide what to say on the label. Rule lines on paper and pencil out the words. Try different sizes of writing.

**2** When each line is decided, cut the lines into strips for easy rearrangement on a new sheet of paper. Either rule a vertical center line or a line to left or right to justify the beginning or end of the lines.

**3** When happy with the layout, glue the strips in place, ensuring they're straight, then ink over them. Place this sheet under the label fabric and trace off.

## Making a Hanging Sleeve

This type of tubular sleeve protects your quilt from splinters that may come off a wooden hanging pole.

- Attach the sleeve after the quilt is finished and bound. Sleeves are often made from leftover backing fabric. Or choose a plain fabric so you can write the labeling information on it.
- Measure the width of your quilt. Cut a piece of fabric to the width x 9 inches. Press in ¼ inch twice at both short ends, and sew.

- Fold in half lengthwise, wrong sides together, and sew the long edge with a ⅝-inch seam. Center the seam and press open.
- With the pressed seam against the back of the quilt, center the sleeve horizontally at the top. Slipstitch to the back of the quilt down the long edges. Also stitch the lower layer of the short ends to the backing to ensure the hanging pole slips into the attached tube, rather than behind it, next to the quilt back.

**Left:** Detail of Album quilt, American, nineteenth century. In this quilt each block has been elaborately labeled by its maker.

**Above:** Example of a hanging sleeve with label. The arrow indicates the position of the pole.

# PATCHWORK TECHNIQUES

Patchwork, or piecing, involves sewing together pieces of fabric into patterns, by hand or machine. Born of necessity, as a way of extending the life of precious fabrics in times when the process of cloth making was long and arduous, patchwork has developed over the centuries, especially in America, into a hugely popular craft.

The perishable nature of textiles makes it difficult to ascertain how long patchwork has been practiced, but the universality of geometric pattern means that in more than one place and culture, people have translated small fabric shapes into a larger design for functional or decorative purposes.

In eighteenth-century England, the arrival of colorful Indian chintz brought a fashion for bedcovers pieced with a single repeating unit. The hexagon, pieced over paper templates, was the preferred working shape, and this method became known as English patchwork. The art of patchwork based on block construction developed in America. Working in blocks is efficient in both materials and labor, demanding neither long periods of free time, nor a large working space. The wonderful variety of designs and the inventiveness of the pattern names show that no matter how simple their tools, early quilt-makers were as creative as today's stitchers.

**Left:** Detail of *Baskets* with chintz border, American, 1860–70.

# LIBRARY OF PIECED BLOCKS

Choosing which block design to make can be difficult. There are more than 1,000 recorded pieced-block patterns to choose from, and of course you can always design your own. The greater the number of pieces in the block, the longer the cutting and piecing will take, and beginners should avoid blocks with too many pieces. The size of your finished project should also be taken into consideration when deciding on a block design. For ease of sewing, the block size should relate to the grid of your block pattern. For example, four-patch designs work well on 4-, 8-, and 12-inch blocks; nine-patch designs on 3-, 6-, 9-, and 12-inch blocks.

Do not be surprised to learn that the same design is known by two or more names or that the same name applies to several different block patterns. Before the great revival of quilt making in the 1970s and the formal identification of block designs, blocks were named by the people who stitched them. Sometimes pattern names were incorrectly remembered or simply rechristened to reflect events and circumstances closer to the maker. There are sixty pieced designs in this chapter to choose from as a possible starting point. The blocks in the library follow the custom of organizing them according to the underlying grid over which the design has been drafted.

## One-patch Designs

One-patch designs are created by an aggregation of multiples of the same single units.

Stars made with diamonds

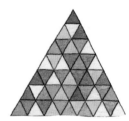

Thousand Pyramids made with triangles

Grandmother's Flower Garden made with hexagons

Brick Wall made with rectangles

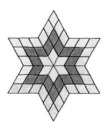

Radiating Star made with diamonds

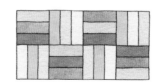

Rail Fence made with rectangles

Streak of Lightning made with triangles

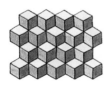

Tumbling Blocks made with diamonds

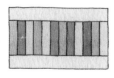

Chinese Coins made with rectangles

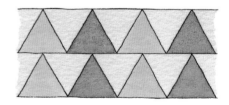

Land of Pharaohs made with triangles

# Four-patch Designs

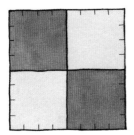

Four-patch

Variable Star

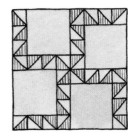

Postage Stamp Baskets

Pinwheel

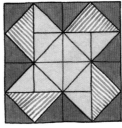

July 4th

Century

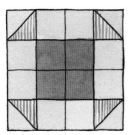

Puss in the Corner

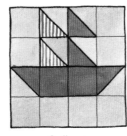

Dutchman's Puzzle

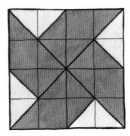

Bow Tie

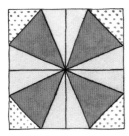

Kaleidoscope

Sailboat

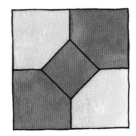

Whirlwind

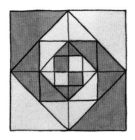

Monkey Wrench

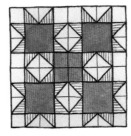

Devil's Claw

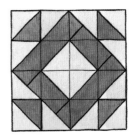

Broken Dishes

# Five-patch Designs

Five-patch

Sister's Choice

Broken Arrows

Jack in the Box

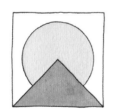

Cake Stand

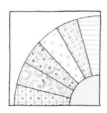

Lady of the Lake

# Seven-patch Designs

Hemstitch

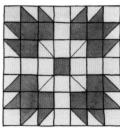

Peony

Stonemason's Puzzle

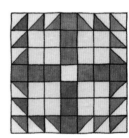

Bear's Paw

Lincoln's Platform

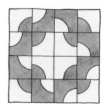

Hens and Chickens

# Curved-seam Designs

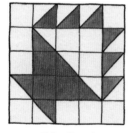

Moon Over the Mountain

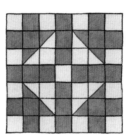

Fan

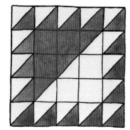

Dresden Plate

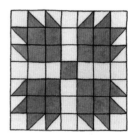

Dove at the Window

Mariner's Compass

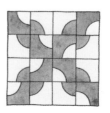

Orange Peel

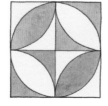

Drunkard's Path

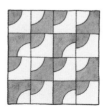

Falling Timbers

# Nine-patch Designs

Nine-patch

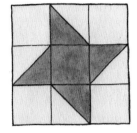

Friendship Star

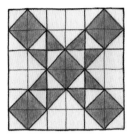

Cats and Mice

Shoo Fly

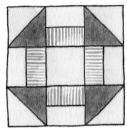

Churn Dash

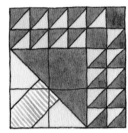

Pine Tree

Card Trick

Pennsylvania

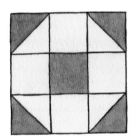

Nine-patch Snowball

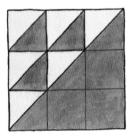

Birds in the Air

Ohio Star

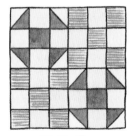

Tic Tac Toe

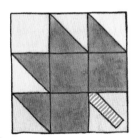

Maple Leaf

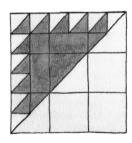

Sawtooth

Prairie Queen

# SPEED-PIECING

Quick piecing methods that make effective use of rotary-cutting equipment and the sewing machine are ideal for sewing numbers of identical units. The geometric nature of many patterns means that various combinations of strip-pieced squares and rectangles and pieced half-square triangles can be used to reduce the time taken to work sets of blocks.

## STRIPS INTO SQUARES

In this technique, different colored fabric strips are joined in alternating bands, cut into strips, and sewn together to make alternate-color patchwork blocks.

### Two-color Nine-patch Blocks

① Sew a pieced strip, using one color in the middle and one other color on both sides (set 1). Press seams to the center. Stitch the second strip from the opposite end. Sew a second pieced strip (set 2) twice the length of set 1, reversing the colors. Press seams outward.

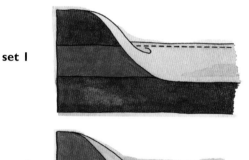

② Cross-cut these into slices of the required width.

③ Matching seams carefully, machine sew the slices in the correct order to make the nine-patch block.

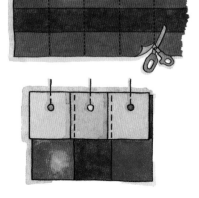

### Three-color Nine-patch Blocks

① Sew together two pieced strips of your required width, following the illustrations below.

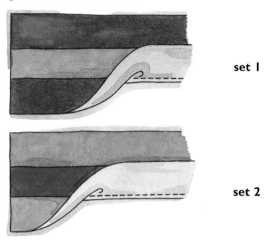

set 1

set 2

② Cross-cut the pieced strips and sew the slices together to make your nine-patch block.

### Four-color Nine-patch Blocks

① Sew together two pieced strips of your required width, following the illustrations.

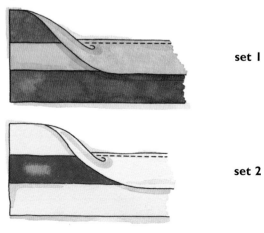

set 1

set 2

② Cross-cut and sew the slices together.

# double nine-patch   **made by Linda Maltman**

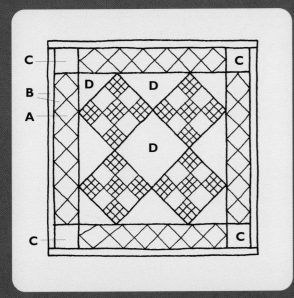

## MATERIALS
- 1¼ yd. backing
- 1¼ yd. 60-in.-wide batting
- ¼ yd. red print A for border
- ⅞ yd. solid red B for border fabric and binding
- ¼ yd. red print C for border corner squares
- ½ yd. solid blue D for center square and side triangles
- ½ yd. equivalent mixed yellow prints for double nine-patch blocks
- ½ yd. equivalent blue prints for corner double nine-patch blocks
- Matching sewing and quilting threads

**Finished size** 36 x 36 in.
**Block size** 9 x 9 in.
**Number of blocks** 5

## CUTTING
### FABRIC A
- Cut 24 squares, each 3½ in.

### FABRIC B
- Cut two strips, each 1½ x 38 in., and two strips, each 1½ x 36 in., for the outer border.
- For the binding, cut strips 1½ in. wide (½ in. finished width) for a total of 150 in. when joined.
- Cut 10 squares, each 5⅝ in., and divide twice diagonally to make 40 side triangles for square-on-point border. These will have the straight grain of the fabric on the long side of the triangle to make a stable edge to the quilt.
- Cut eight squares, each 3⅛ in., and divide once diagonally to make 16 corner triangles for the square-on-point border. These will have the straight grain running around the right-angle corner of the triangle, also to give a stable edge to the border.
- Cut four strips, 1½ in. wide and 7 in. long, for the center nine-patch blocks.

### FABRIC C
- Cut four squares, each 4¾ in.

### FABRIC D
- Cut one square, 14 in., and divide twice diagonally to make four side triangles.
- Cut one square, 9½ in., for the center square.
- Cut two squares, each 8½ in., and divide once diagonally for corner side triangles.

### MIXED YELLOW PRINTS
- Cut four strips, each 1½ in. wide x 26 in. long, or equivalent length.
- Cut five strips, each 1½ in. wide x 7 in. long, for the nine-patch blocks.

### BLUE PRINT SCRAPS
- Cut 16 squares, each 3½ in.
- Cut five strips, each 1½ in. wide x 26 in. long, or equivalent length.

## Sewing

### To make the blue and yellow nine-patch blocks

1 Using an accurate ¼-in. seam allowance, sew the yellow and blue strips into two different set 1 combinations, and one set 2, with a different yellow print in each position. Press seams toward the blue.

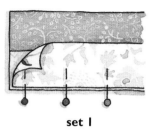 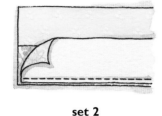

**set 1**      **set 2**

2 Cross-cut into 16 slices, each 1½-in. wide. If using a rotary cutter, match a printed grid line with the horizontal seam of the set to keep the cut end at right angles to the seams. If this end of the fabric "drifts," true it up again before proceeding.

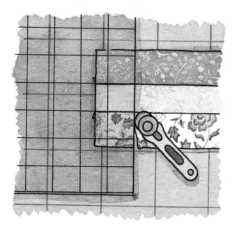

3 Sew one slice from set 2 between two set 1 slices, one from each fabric pairing. Press and check that each block measures 3½ × 3½ in., including a ¼-in. seam allowance.

**set 1**      **set 2**      **set 3**

### To make the red and yellow nine-patch blocks

1 Similarly, sew the yellow and red 7-in. strips into two different set 1s and one set 2, with a different yellow print in each position. Press the seems toward the red.

2 Cross-cut each set into four slices, each 1½-in. wide. Sew one slice from set 2 between two set 1 slices, one from each fabric pairing. Each should measure 3½ × 3½ in., including a ¼-in. seam.

  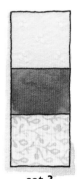

**set 1**      **set 2**      **set 3**

### To make the double nine-patch blocks

1 Arrange the center and corner pieced nine-patches with the unpieced blue print squares between. Sew these units together in rows. Sew the three rows together to complete four blocks, 9½-in. square including seams.

### To make the pieced border

1 Attach one side triangle to two opposite sides of 16 border A squares as shown (fig. 1). To the remaining eight A squares, add one side triangle and two corner triangles as shown (fig. 2).

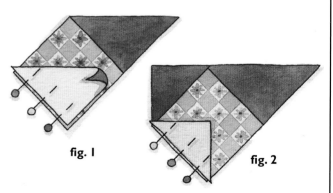

**fig. 1**      **fig. 2**

2 Arrange the prepared units into four borders, each having four step 1 units in the center with a step 2 unit at both ends. Assemble the borders by sewing the remaining diagonal seams.

**Above:** *Double Nine-Patch*, by Linda Maltman, English, twentieth century.

## Assembling the top

1 Arrange the double nine-patch blocks, with D fabric center square, side triangles, and corner triangles. Sew in diagonal rows.

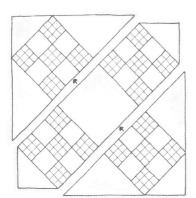

2 Sew one pieced border strip to opposite sides of the quilt. Attach a corner C square to both ends of the remaining two borders. Press, then attach to the top and bottom of the quilt.

3 Sew the two shorter outer border strips to the sides and trim as necessary. Add the two long outer border strips to the top and bottom.

## Finishing

1 Mark wreath motif in the center square, rosettes in the four corner squares and the melon-seed pattern in the border squares (see page 185).

2 Layer, then quilt, using a rectangular grid in the nine-patches. Quilt the wreath pattern. To finish, bind the quilt using separate continuous binding (see page 50).

**Above:** *Bear's Paw*, American Amish, ca. 1920.

# HALF-SQUARE TRIANGLES

Working with triangles requires dealing with bias seams, which are not stable and are likely to stretch during cutting and sewing. Multiple distorted edges make precision piecing difficult. This method ensures greater speed and improved accuracy.

## Piecing Half-square Triangles

**1** On the wrong side of the lighter of the two fabrics, mark the required-size square, then rule one diagonal. Place your two fabric squares right sides together.

**2** Using the pencil line as your guide, accurately sew ¼ in. away on both sides of the diagonal.

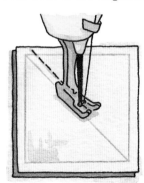

**3** Following the marked pencil line, cut out the square, then cut the diagonal along the pencil line.

**4** Press the seam allowance toward the darker fabric and open to a square.

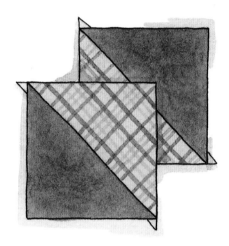

**5** For making multiple half-square triangle units, mark the lighter of your two fabrics with a grid of squares. Mark the diagonals in neighboring squares in opposite directions. Follow the diagram below for sewing directions.

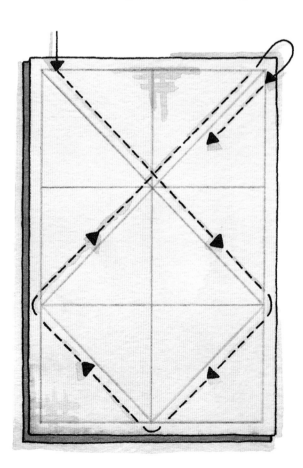

# crown of thorns

## MATERIALS
- 2¼ yd. backing
- 85 x 85 in. (minimum) batting
- 5 yd. black
- 2½ yd. pink
- Matching sewing and quilting threads

**Finished size** 74 x 74 in.
**Block size** 10 x 10 in.
**Number of pieced blocks** 16

## CUTTING
### BLACK
- For the borders, cut strips 7½ in. x fabric width. Join to make borders 76 in. long for the top and bottom. Cut strips 7½ in. wide to make two borders 62 in. long for the sides.
- For the side triangles, cut three squares, each 17 in., and divide diagonally both ways to make 12 triangles.
- For the corner triangles, cut two squares, each 10½ in., and divide each once diagonally.
- Cut nine setting squares, each 10½ in.
- Cut strips 2½ in. wide, then cross-cut to make 80 squares. First use up scraps remaining from cutting the preceding pieces before cutting into the main piece.
- The remaining black pieces will be cut later.

### PINK
- Cut strips 2 in. wide across the width of the fabric to total 8½ yd. for binding.
- For the inner border, cut strips 2 in. wide. Join to make four borders, each 62 in. long.
- Cut 64 squares, each 2½ in.
- The remaining pink squares will be cut later.

## Sewing

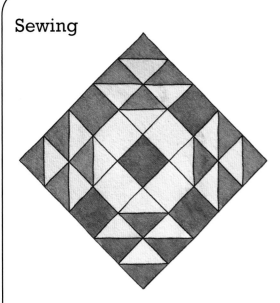

**3** Arrange the blocks with the plain sashing squares, the large side triangles and the corner triangles. Assemble into diagonal rows. Press seams away from pieced blocks and join the rows to complete.

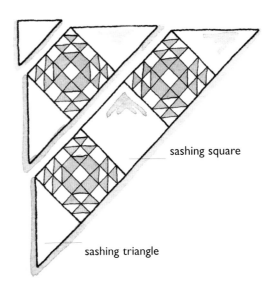

sashing square

sashing triangle

**1** Sixteen half-square-triangle units are required per block. Therefore, each block requires a grid of eight squares, each 2⅞ in., to be marked on the wrong side of the pink fabric. Mark 16 such grids, one per block. Place right sides together with similarly sized pieces of black and turn into half-square-triangle units as directed on page 69. Press carefully.

**2** Arrange these units with the plain squares of black and pink to make 16 crown of thorns blocks. Sew units into rows; sew rows into blocks.

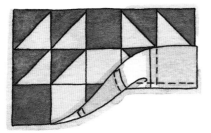

**4** Attach the inner pink borders with straight-cut corners (see page 43). Sew the short black borders to the sides and add the longer ones top and bottom.

## Finishing

**1** Mark the quilting design in the borders, side blocks and triangles—a cable for the border, a wreath in the side blocks, and a floral motif in the side triangles.

**2** Layer and baste the quilt (see page 47). Quilt, starting at the center, and work outward. The crown of thorns blocks are quilted with a diagonal grid, which can be worked using masking tape.

**3** Following the directions for automatic miters on page 50, use the 2-in. wide strips to bind the quilt. The finished binding is ½ in. on the front.

**4** Sign and date your quilt to finish (see page 55).

**Above:** *Flying Geese,* American, early nineteenth century.

# FLYING GEESE

The Flying Geese unit is a pieced unit whose shape is a rectangle divided into one large triangle (the goose) and two small ones (the sky).

## Making a Flying Geese Unit

❶ From the goose fabric, cut one square. From the sky fabric, cut four smaller squares. To determine the size of the goose square, add 1¼ in. to the desired finished width of the flying geese units. The sky squares are the height of the unit (always half of the width) plus ⅞ in. For example, to make a 2 × 4-in. unit, the goose square must measure 5¼ × 5¼ in. and the sky squares, 2⅞ × 2⅞ in.

❷ On the right side of the goose square, rule both diagonals. On the wrong side of the sky squares, rule one diagonal.

❸ With the goose square right side up, position a small sky square, right side down, in the two opposite corners, lining up the drawn diagonals. Pin, then trim the tiny triangles from where the two squares overlap in the middle.

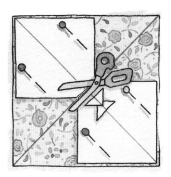

❹ Attach the two small squares to the large square by sewing ¼ in. away from the drawn diagonal on both sides of the line.

❺ Cut along the diagonal between the stitching to yield two units.

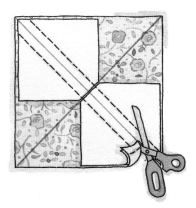

❻ Press the sky squares away from the seam.

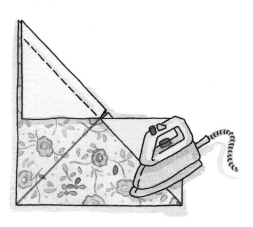

❼ Place another sky square as shown in step 8, again matching the diagonal, and stitch along both sides of the diagonal ¼ in. away as before. Repeat for the second unit.

❽ Cut apart between the stitching to make four geese units.

## Flying Geese variations

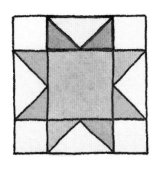

Variable Star                    Virginia Reel

# flying geese
**made by Veronika Smith**

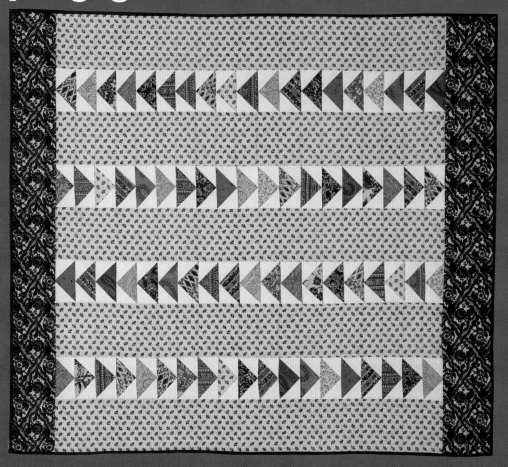

## MATERIALS
- 1½ yd. backing
- 1½ yd. batting
- 1¼ yd. vertical border print used for the two shortest sides. If cut across the fabric, ⅜ yd. is sufficient.
- 1¼ yd. setting fabric
- ½ yd. muslin for sky pieces
- ½ yd. equivalent mixed prints for geese, none less than 5½-in. square
- ¼ yd. contrast solid color for ¼-in. finished binding
- Matching sewing and quilting thread

**Finished size** 41 x 48 in.

## CUTTING
### BORDER PRINT
- Being careful to feature the printed design correctly on the strips, cut two strips for the borders for the shortest sides, each 5½ x 43 in. If necessary, modify the width to accommodate the print to the best advantage.

### SETTING FABRIC
- Cut five strips, each 5½ x 40 in., for the vertical setting strips and side borders.

### CONTRAST SOLID
- Cut strips for the binding 1 in. wide, totaling a length of 5¼ in. when joined.

### SKY FABRIC
- Cut 76 squares, each 2⅞ in.

### MIXED GEESE FABRICS
- Cut 19 squares, each 5¼ in. Our example used one square of 19 different prints, but fabrics may be repeated.

## Sewing

1 Following steps 1–7 on page 73, make 19 sets of four geese.

2 Divide the geese into four piles, one of each fabric in each pile if you use 19 different prints. Mix up the geese within the piles so that the same fabric will not always appear in the same place in a column.

3 To center the points of the geese, lightly finger-crease at the center of the long edge of a goose panel.

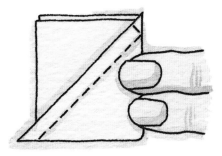

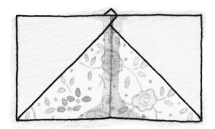

4 Sew the geese into four columns of 19. Use a consistent ¼-in. seam allowance to make sure the tip of the goose triangle exactly meets the base of the next triangle. Center this point to the base of the next goose. Press the seams carefully.

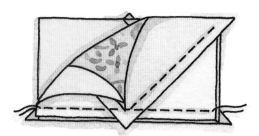

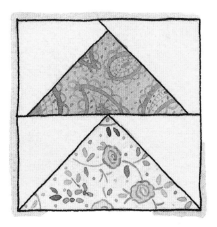

5 Sew the vertical strips of setting fabric and the columns of geese together alternately. Press before adding the borders to the shortest sides.

## Finishing

1 Make a template of the goose triangle and mark the vertical setting strips with a succession of triangles, then quilt.

2 Quilt the geese in-the-ditch. For the borders along the shortest sides, quilt following the printed design.

3 Bind using single binding with automatic miters (see page 50).

**Above:** *String of Flags*, American, early nineteenth century.

# RECTANGLES

The following instructions allow you to seam on the correct bias angle of the rectangle being used. It also keeps the grain parallel with the block sides. It is a fast method and, unlike some quick-piecing techniques, it is very economical in terms of the amount of fabric required.

**1** On paper, draw a rectangle of the required size. Divide it diagonally once. Make a cardboard template of the triangle without seam allowances. This will be used to cut the fabric at the correct angle.

**2** Make a second template in clear plastic of the whole rectangle, including ¼-in. outer seam allowances. Mark the diagonal seam on this template, noting that the diagonal seam line will not coincide with the template corners when projected into the seam allowances.

**3** Place two pieces of fabric right sides up, the lighter one on top. Work on a cutting mat. If the mat is too small, work step 4 on a table. Rule pencil lines, then cut with scissors.

**4** Position the cardboard triangle template right way up, with its right-angle corner to the right-angle corner of the fabric. Place your ruler against the diagonal of the triangle so that the other side of the ruler reaches the top corner of the fabric. If the ruler does not reach the top of the fabric, slide the ruler and the template together across the fabric, keeping the lower edge of the template level with the lower fabric edge until they do. Cut or rule a line at this point to establish your working edge. The cardboard triangle is no longer needed.

**5** Cut off the fabric corner. Using the diagonal as the bias guide will enable you to cut strips at the correct angle to make rectangles on the grain. From the edge just established, cut strips the width of the short sides of the rectangle plus 1 in. For example, for a finished rectangle measuring 5½ x 8 in., cut strips 6½ in. wide.

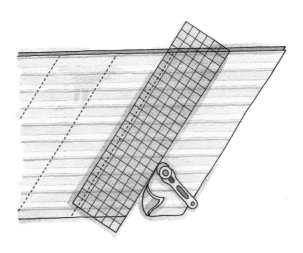

**6** Sew the strips, right sides together, in pairs, one of each fabric, offsetting one against the other by ¼ in. at the start of the seam. This ensures that the fabric is level when opened out. Press, then sew the pairs together again, continuing to alternate the fabrics, until all are joined into a single pieced fabric.

**7** Place the pieced fabric right side up and position the rectangle template over it, aligning the diagonal ruled on the template with the first seam, as near to one corner as possible. Draw around the template. Slide the template along the seam until it just clears the first rectangle marked, then continue to mark and cut rectangles.

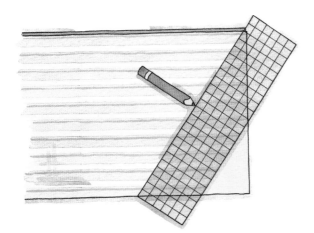

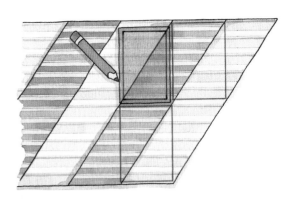

**Above:** *Blazing Star*, American, early nineteenth century.

# DIAMONDS

The eight-point Star of Bethlehem on page 80 is made up of seven rows with seven diamonds in each star point. Seven sets of seven strips are sewn, and from each set eight diagonal slices are cut, one for each star point.

**1** Arrange seven fabric strips in the required color sequence to make up seven sets.

**2** With right sides together and taking a ¼-in. seam allowance, pin, then sew the strips into sets, staggering each strip by its width as shown in the illustration below. Press all sets carefully.

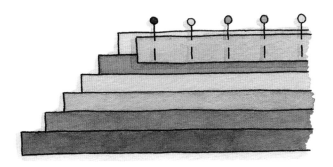

**3** Place one set on the cutting mat. Position a quilter's ruler with the 45° angle along one of the seams and trim the staggered edge before cutting slices to the required width.

**4** Cross-cut into slices of the required width.

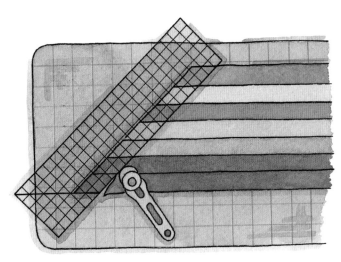

**5** Sort the slices into the required color sequence. With right sides facing and taking ¼-in. seams, sew together, matching the internal seams as accurately as possible. Take care not to stretch the seams while pressing.

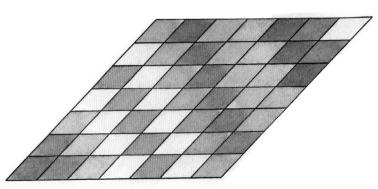

# star of bethlehem
## made by Veronika Smith

## MATERIALS

- 2 yd. muslin or sheeting for backing, 70-in. wide
- 85 x 85 in. (minimum) batting
- 2 yd. red
- 1½ yd. violet
- 1 yd. navy
- ½ yd. each turquoise, green, dark green, and lilac
- ¼ yd. each dark violet and peach
- Scrap of light blue
- Matching sewing threads and medium blue quilting thread

**Finished size 64 x 64 in.**

## CUTTING

- Cut strips, each 25 x 1⅞ in., in the following colors and quantities:

| | |
|---|---|
| (A) light blue x 1 | (B) dark violet x 3 |
| (C) navy x 3 | (D) turquoise x 7 |
| (E) green x 5 | (F) dark green x 8 |
| (G) violet x 7 | (H) lilac x 6 |
| (I) red x 5 | (J) peach x 4 |

## NAVY

- Cut one square, 21 in., and divide on both diagonals for the side triangles.
- Cut four corner squares, each 14½ in.

## VIOLET

- Cut two strips 61½ x 6½ in. and two strips 48½ x 6½ in.

## RED

- Cut straight-grain strips 1½-in.-wide to total 264 in. long for the binding.

## Sewing

1 Arrange the strips in the color sequences shown below and sew into seven sets, staggering each strip by its width (see step 3 on page 79).

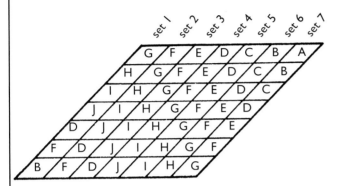

2 Cross-cut each set into eight slices 1⅞ in. wide. Do not rush this step. Watch for any drifting and always true up the angle before proceeding.

3 Arrange the slices into their correct sequence and sew together to make the eight points of the star.

4 Arrange the star and sew the points together in pairs, matching the seams; stop sewing ¼ in. from the outer end. Following the instructions on page 84, inset a corner square between the points.

5 Sew two pairs of points together; stop sewing ¼ in. away from the raw edge. Inset a triangle between them.

6 With right sides together and matching center seams, sew the two halves together (for advice on eight-seam joints see page 88). Stop sewing ¼ in. from the end to allow for insetting the remaining two side triangles.

7 Sew the two shorter violet border strips to opposite sides of the quilt. Add the longer strips to the quilt top and bottom.

8 The sawtooth border needs 120 pieced half-square-triangle units in red and violet. Follow the directions on page 69 for speed-piecing these units. Begin by marking out grids to a total of 60 squares, each 2⅞ x 2⅞ in. on the wrong side of the red. Assemble the pieced squares into two strips of 29 squares and two strips of 31 squares. Attach the shorter strips of the sawtooth border with the violet teeth toward the center of the quilt. Add the longer strips to match.

## Finishing

1 Mark the quilting design with wreaths in the navy setting squares and triangles, and with the cable in the violet inner border.

2 Layer the quilt (see page 47). Quilt in-the-ditch beginning with concentric diamonds in the points of the star. Work outward to the wreaths and cable border.

3 Trim the edges of the quilt and finish with red binding using your preferred method (for binding, see page 48).

# SEMINOLE PATCHWORK

Attributed to the Seminole Indians of Florida, Seminole patchwork is a variation of strip-piecing. It is generally worked with narrow strips of solid-color fabrics sewn into sets, then cross-cut and reassembled into a variety of patterns. The patterns are frequently extremely intricate and require accuracy in matching and sewing seams. The traditional colorful geometric bands of pattern lend themselves to strong horizontal arrangements, generally spaced with unpieced strips of varied widths. The close proximity of seam allowances means that Seminole projects are usually lined but not quilted.

## Making Seminole Patterns

The best way to discover the diversity of patterns possible with this technique is to experiment. At first, practice with 1½-in. strips with ¼-in. seam allowances. After trying these patterns, experiment with your own ideas. Different patterns use different amounts of fabric. Since this technique does not use fabric economically, if you want to make something of a specific size, a sample is essential to ensure that you have enough fabric for your project.

❶ Load your machine with a neutral-color sewing thread and set a short stitch length, about 15 per inch, to prevent the slices from coming unstitched when cross-cut.

❷ Follow the basic instructions to work sets of strips as given for the Double Nine-patch quilt (see page 64), and try some of the more common patterns given below.

### Two-color checkerboard

Press the seam allowances on the assembled pair of contrasting strips toward the darker fabric. Cross-cut into slices. Turn alternate slices to bring the lower color to the top. Sew the slices together in pairs, right sides together and using the interlocking seams (see page 37) to make a good match in the center.

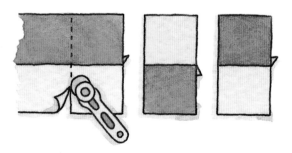

### Square on-point

Assemble a set of three strips, using either two or three colors but with the most eye-catching color in the middle. Cross-cut into slices. When joining, offset the top slice so that the first seam aligns with the second seam on the slice below.

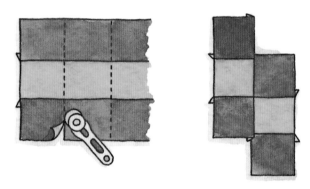

Repeat this offset when sewing the pairs of slices together. The pieced band will have a stepped edge. Do not trim until the neighboring unpieced strip is sewn onto each side.

**Above right:** Detail of *Seminole Wall Hanging*, by Judith Gill, twentieth century.

## Diamonds

Assemble a set of three strips with a contrast center and slightly wider outer strips. Use a quilter's ruler to make the first cut at a 45° angle to the outer edges. Then cut slices of a consistent width parallel to this edge.

## Chevrons

Assemble two identical sets of three strips. The outer strips should be slightly wider than the center strip. On the first set, use a quilter's ruler to make the first cut, sloping to the left at a 45° angle to the edges. Continue to cut slices from this sloping edge. On the second set of strips, make the 45° angle cut slope to the right, then cut slices the same size as for the first set. Pair one slice from each set.

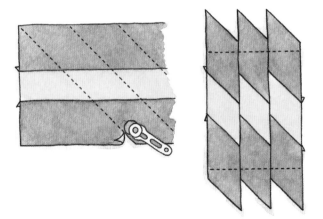

Sew the strips together to form diamonds of contrasting color. The jagged edge will be trimmed when the band is joined to the next strips.

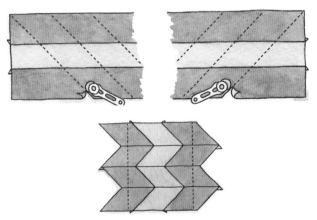

# INSETTING

Insetting is required when you have to sew a piece into an angled space made by the joining of two other pieces. Popular block designs requiring insetting include Bow Ties, Cactus Baskets, and many of the star and diamond patterns. Each side of the inset is sewn separately, so hand sewing is frequently preferred. However, insetting can be done successfully by machine.

## Insetting by Machine

With this method, the seam is sewn from the center outward in two separate halves to ensure that no tucks appear at the center.

**1** Mark dots and seam line as for step 1 of Insetting by Hand (see facing page).

**2** With pieces right sides together, pin through the dots. Pin the rest of the seam at right angles to the stitching line.

**3** Set the machine to stitch length to 0. Place the patches under the machine with the seam allowances facing to the back, and manually turn the balance wheel to insert the machine needle into the inset point, removing the pin as you do so. Hold the thread ends to one side and sew two or three stitches—this will lock the seam. Stop, then reset to a normal straight stitch length and continue sewing the seam.

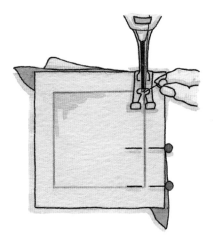

**4** Remove the pieces from the machine and check the seam.

**5** Fold the pieced unit to one side; this allows you to match the second half of the seam. Start with a pin at the inset point but now fold the seams the other way. Pin in place.

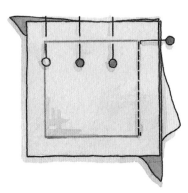

**6** As in step 3, set the machine to stitch length 0, then complete the seam.

**7** Remove the work from the machine, check the seams, and press carefully.

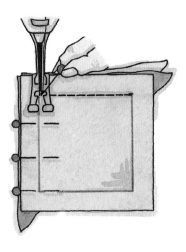

**Above:** Detail of *Cactus Baskets*, American, early nineteenth century.

## Insetting by Hand

**1** Mark with dots exactly where the inset will be joined. Mark seam lines on the wrong side of the fabric.

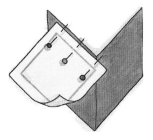

**2** With right sides together and the inset piece on top, pin through the dots to match inset points. Match seams on one side from the inner corner to one end. Pin the seam.

**3** Starting at the outer corner, make a small backstitch to secure and sew the pieces together; use a short running stitch until you reach the inset points. Secure with a backstitch.

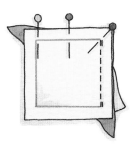

**4** Remove the pins and fold the pieced unit below to one side, which allows you to match up the rest of the seam to the end. Pin, making sure that there is no tuck at the inner angle.

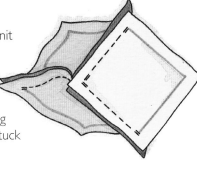

**5** Without sewing into the seam allowance, complete the seam with a running stitch.

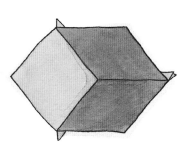

**Above:** *Drunkard's Path*, American, nineteenth century.

# CURVED-SEAM PIECING

Curved seams have the reputation of being difficult to sew. Careful cutting out and preparation are just part of the solution; the rest lies in not stretching or distorting those curved edges. The best results come from doing it carefully and right the first time, as any resewing of seams leads to over-handling and problems of distortion. Common curved-seam blocks include Moon Over the Mountain, New York Beauty, and pieced fan designs.

## Making a Drunkard's Path Block

① Using the Drunkard's Path block template on page 174, cut out A and B. Draw a sewing line ¼ in. from the raw edge on the wrong side of both pieces to be joined. The curved edges should have a center balance mark or notch, as shown. Matching these helps distribute the fabric evenly around the curve. These must be exactly opposite each other when the two curves are together. If working with long curves or when making large blocks, add extra marks equally spaced around the curves.

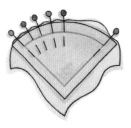

② Place the two curved pieces right sides together and spear the central notches with a pin as shown below. The two curves appear as if they will never come together, as they face opposite directions.

③ With pins, locate both ends of the seam, exactly matching the ¼-in. seam allowance.

④ Two curves will fit together perfectly at only one point—where the seam line is drawn. If the seam deviates even a little, one side will be longer, or shorter, than it should be, so stay exactly on the drawn lines. Work on one half of the curve at a time. Put a pin halfway between the center and the corner on the seam line and push it through the piece below, also on the seam line. Repeat, putting pins halfway between the spaces until the gaps between pins are no greater than about ¼ in. Repeat to ease together the other half of the seam. Baste.

⑤ Sew the seam carefully. Some people like to hand sew curves, but machine sewing is faster and, with practice, just as accurate. If machine sewing, turn the curve smoothly and stay on the line. Use a short stitch length to create more "give" and prolong the life of the curved seam.

⑥ After sewing, inspect both sides. There should be no little bubbles or tucks. If the seam looks good, return to the wrong side and clip into the convex curve at regular intervals almost to the seam. Press.

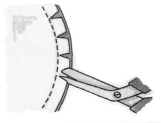

**TIP**
● Some quilters prefer to clip the convex curve before pinning and sewing. However, with this method it is easy to sew through the end of a clip by accident. It can also distort that side of the seam, making it very hard to match the curves.

# EIGHT-SEAM JOINT

Some of the most challenging quilt blocks contain shapes that meet in multiple joints. An eight-seam joint appears in such traditional block designs as Mariner's Compass, Kaleidoscope, and Dutchman's Puzzle. With many converging seams, the join requires careful and accurate sewing. The instructions given below are for sewing an eight-seam joint on a pinwheel block, but the technique applies to any block pattern with multiple joints.

## Making a Block with an Eight-seam Joint

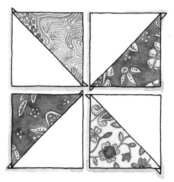

**1** Arrange your basic components to make the block configuration as above—in this case, a pinwheel block. Make sure the pressed seam allowances in all four quarter-blocks rotate in one direction.

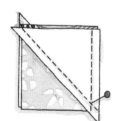

The wrong side of the top half of the pinwheel block

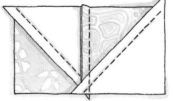

The wrong side of the bottom half of the pinwheel block

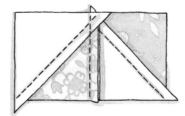

**Right:** Detail of *Snow Crystals*, American, ca.1920.

**2** Sew the half-square triangles together in pairs, matching the seam intersections.

**3** After sewing two halves of the block, spear the centers with a pin, even if the ends of the seams are not exactly level. It is more important to have the centers match exactly than to have the edges of the blocks level. Pin at right angles across the whole seam and remove the spear pin before stitching.

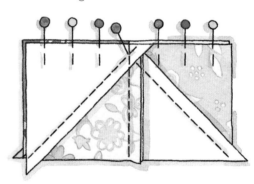

**4** To check how good the match is, machine baste about 1 in. of stitching through the center joint, using the longest stitch possible on the machine. Large basting stitches are easy to remove if the centers do not match precisely. If you are happy with the appearance of the seam, adjust the stitch length to normal (10–12 per inch) and sew the seam slowly and carefully.

**5** If you are sewing by hand, fold all the seam allowances in the same direction, swirling them in the middle to reduce bulk (see page 36). If machine sewing, press the seams flat, with the final seam pressed open.

# pinwheel variation

**made by Peggy Bell**

## MATERIALS
- 1¾ yd. 60-in.-wide backing
- 1¾ yd. 60-in.-wide batting
- 1⅜ yd. white
- ½ yd. navy for binding and border
- 1¾ yd. total of mixed navy-and-white prints with a minimum of three different fabrics
- Matching sewing and quilting thread

**Finished size**  52½ x 52½ in.
**Block size**  12 x 12 in. and 4 x 4 in.
**Number of blocks**  4 large and 53 small

## CUTTING
### NAVY
- Cut strips 4½ in. wide and seam together to make two border strips 55 in. long and two strips 48 in. long.
- Cut five strips 1 in. wide across the full width of the fabric and join into a continuous length for the binding.

### MIXED NAVY-AND-WHITE PRINTS
- Cut four 6⅞-in. squares and divide diagonally to make eight triangles.
- Cut four 2⅞-in. squares and divide once diagonally to make eight triangles.

### WHITE
- Cut as for mixed navy-and-white prints.
- For the pinwheel blocks, the rest of the cutting will be done after sewing.

## Sewing

1 To make the large pinwheel blocks, draw 12 squares, each 6⅞ in., in grids on the wrong side of the white fabric. Plan the grids to fit sensibly with the print fabrics being used. It will be more interesting if a different number of each print are worked. Mark one diagonal in each square, with diagonals going in opposite directions in adjacent squares.

2 Place the white fabric on the navy-and-white print with right sides together and begin making the half-square-triangle units (see page 69).

3 Press the seam allowances toward the dark fabric. Set aside eight of the prepared half-square units for the side triangles.

4 Arrange the remaining 16 units into four groups of four. Have them turned the right way to form the large pinwheel and sew together into blocks.

5 Make up eight side setting triangles by sewing one large white and one large navy-and-white print triangle to two adjacent sides of the eight units set aside earlier.

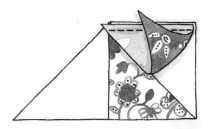

6 To make the small pinwheel blocks, begin by marking out a total of 108 squares, each 2⅞ in., in conveniently sized grids on the wrong side of the white fabric. Work the pieced half-square triangles and press carefully before assembling sets of four to make 53 small pinwheel blocks.

7 To the remaining four small pieced units, add one small white and one small navy-and-white print triangle to two adjacent sides, maintaining the checkered effect. These units fit at the ends of the pieced setting strips, midway along the sides of the quilt.

8 Sew the remaining small triangles in pairs of one white and one navy-and-white print to make the quarter units for the ends of the pieced setting strips at the corners of the quilt.

9 Arrange and sew the quilt blocks as shown below. Check that the side and corner triangles at the ends of the setting strips are correctly placed to form straight sides to the quilt.

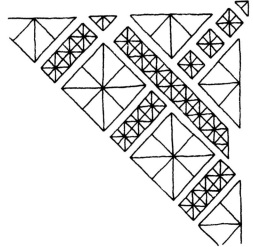

10 To attach the straight-cut border, sew the shorter strips to two opposite sides of the quilt first, then add the long strips to the top and bottom (see page 43).

## Finishing

1 Mark the quilt top with broken curves for large pinwheels, cable for border, and echo pattern for small pinwheels (see patterns on pages 186 and 188).

2 Assemble the quilt layers and baste (see page 47). Quilt starting from the center and work outward.

3 Add a continuous binding with automatic miters (see page 50).

4 Label and and date your quilt to finish (see page 55).

## Log Cabin Variations

By changing the block arrangements, many different quilt designs emerge, all resulting from how the light and dark halves of the block are composed together. Well-known examples include the Barn Raising pattern on page 95, with light and dark concentric diamonds; variations of alternating light and dark smaller squares (above); Straight Furrows (left), where every alternate block creates light and dark diagonals; and Pineapple variations, formed by changing the position of dark and light strips within individual blocks (see page 96).

**Above:** Detail of *Log Cabin*, light and dark variation, American, early nineteenth century.
**Left:** Detail of *Log Cabin*, straight furrows variation, American, early nineteenth century.
**Page 95:** Detail of *Log Cabin*, barn raising variation, American, nineteenth century.

# LOG CABIN

The Log Cabin design, which traveled with the early settlers to the New World, was probably renamed after the traditional pioneer homes. It is a simple pattern made by adding successive strips of fabric around a central unit. Although it is considered a particularly American motif, there are primitive examples of the design as far back as the ancient Egyptians. The block is easy to make, and with limitless design opportunities, it remains a firm favorite among quilt-makers worldwide.

## Making a Log Cabin Block

① From the template on page 174, enlarge the block to 7 in. Trace the block onto a square of muslin.

② Cut a 1½-in. red square and pin or baste right side up to the middle of the foundation.

③ Cut a variety of light and dark strips each 1½ in. wide. Place a light strip right side down over the center red square, with raw edges level. Stitch together, using a ¼-in. seam allowance. Trim away excess strip so that it is even with the center square.

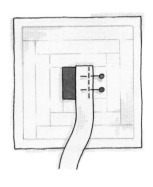 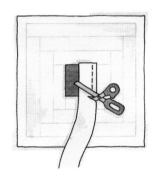

④ Fold the strip right side up and press. Add a second light-colored strip right side down over the center; sew, trim, and press.

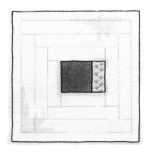 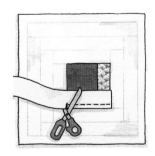

⑤ For the third and fourth strips, choose dark fabrics and attach in the manner outlined in steps 3–6.

⑥ Continue in the same clockwise direction, adding the remaining strips to complete the block.

# barn raising

BEGINNER

## MATERIALS
- 2¼ yd. 80-in.-wide backing
- 85 x 85 in. (minimum) batting
- 2½ yd. red
- 1¾ yd. each pink and white
- 2¼ yd. black

**Finished size** 76 x 76 in.
**Block size** 7 x 7 in.
**Number of blocks** 100

## CUTTING
### RED
- Cut strips 1½ in. wide, joining as necessary to make four outer borders, each 77 in. long.
- Cut strips 1½ in. wide for the logs. From these strips, cut 50 squares, each 1½ in., for the centers.

### PINK
- Cut strips 1½ in. wide, to make four middle borders, each 75 in. long.
- Cut strips 1½ in. wide for logs.

### WHITE
- Cut strips 1½ in. wide, to make four inner borders, each 73 in. long.
- Cut strips 1½ in. wide for logs.

### BLACK
- Cut strips 1½ in. wide for logs. From the strips, cut 50 squares, each 1½ in., for the centers.
- Cut strips 2 in. wide totaling 8½ yd. for a finished ¾-in. binding.

## Sewing

1 Following the instructions on page 93 for making a Log Cabin block, work 50 blocks for each sequence.

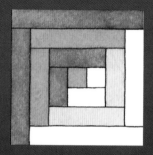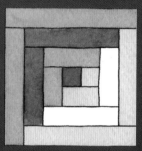

2 Arrange the blocks as illustrated in the photograph opposite, then sew the blocks together in rows. Press, then sew together the rows of blocks.

3 Attach white borders to the sides of the quilt top. Press, then add a white border to top and lower edges. In the same manner, attach the pink and red borders.

4 Layer the quilt (see page 47). Because there are so many seam allowances, Log Cabin designs usually are either quilted in-the-ditch or echo-quilted ¼ in. away from the seams. Quilt around the blocks in long continuous lines up, down, and across the quilt.

5 Trim the backing and batting to ¾ in. beyond the red on all sides. Insert permanent basting just within the seam. Add the binding with a ¼-in. seam, to finish ¾ in. wide. Date and sign your quilt.

# pineapple log cabin · made by Dolly Parker

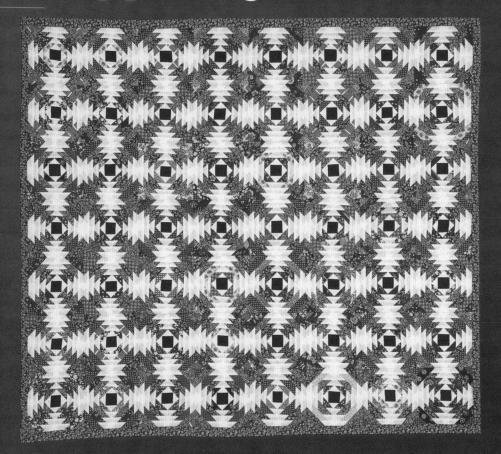

## MATERIALS

- 2 yd. 60-in.-wide backing
- 1 single-bed-size batting (optional)
- 3 yd. white novelty weave
- ¾–1 yd. red/cream print
- 8½ yd. mixed red/white prints
- ¼ yd. red solid
- 2¾ yd. lightweight muslin or thin paper for foundation
- Matching sewing threads

**Finished size** 62½ x 55 in.
**Block size** 7½ x 7½ in.
**Number of blocks** 56

## CUTTING
### MUSLIN OR PAPER

- Enlarge the template on page 174. Cut 56 squares, each 8 in., and mark the foundation grid on each.

### RED SOLID

- Cut 56 squares, each 2 x 2 in.

### WHITE NOVELTY WEAVE

- Cut the fabric into strips, each 1¼ in. wide, for logs.

### MAIN RED/CREAM PRINT

- Cut strips 3 in. wide to total 6¾ yd. for binding and to finish 1¼ in. wide.
- Cut remainder into strips 1¼ in. wide for the logs.

### MIXED RED/WHITE PRINT

- Cut 56 assorted strips, 14 x 1¾ in., for corner strips on blocks (one strip is enough for one block).
- Cut the remaining fabric into strips 1¼ in. wide for the logs.

## Sewing

**1** Pin the center red square to the foundation. Sew white strips to opposite sides of the center as shown below.

**2** Press, then sew strips to top and bottom of the center square (see drawing below).

**3** Change to red print strips, placing them diagonally across the corners of the previous strips with the seam just touching the corners of the red center (see drawing below). Again working opposite sides, attach the strips, press, and trim as you go. Try to use the same fabrics on the round; however, there is no need to use the same fabric in the same place in each block.

**4** Trim away the excess fabric from the previous round of white strips.

**5** Proceed in the same way with the next round of white, again having the seam just touching the corners of the first white round. Press and trim excess fabric from the previous round.

**6** Continue adding red print and white novelty weave rounds alternately.

**7** The true pineapple pattern appears when subsequent seams no longer coincide with those of previous rounds.

**8** When no more white strips can be added, use the 1¾-in.-wide strip of red print to complete the four corners of the block.

**9** Work 56 blocks in this way. If working over paper foundations, tear the paper away before continuing to the next step.

**10** Arrange the blocks in seven rows of eight blocks and sew together into rows. Join the rows to complete the top.

**11** Center the top on the backing and baste together.

## Finishing

**1** Tie the layers together at the block corners as invisibly as possible on the front, using matching thread. Alternatively, machine quilt the main block seams.

**2** Secure the edges with permanent basting within the ¼-in. seam allowance. Trim the backing fabric to 1 in. larger than the edge of the quilt on all sides.

**3** Bind the quilt following the instructions on page 48. Sign and date your quilt to finish (see page 55).

# STRING PIECING

Strings are long, narrow strips of fabric of varying widths, often remnants or scraps from sewing projects. The strings are sewn together to make up a pieced fabric that has the random and asymmetrical appearance of "crazy" patchwork. Anyone who likes the thrifty aspect of patchwork should enjoy this technique, as should quilt-makers who are skilled in exploiting the improvisational aspect of working with a random mix of color and pattern.

Where possible, use similar weight fabrics for the strings and a compatible foundation fabric. Remember to wash all fabrics, including the strings, before sewing. Protect them from fraying by placing them in a mesh bag.

## Making a Sample

1 Collect a mix of fabric strings. Make your own strings from straight fabric strips by cutting down their length at various angles.

2 Any of a variety of foundations, such as thin muslin, can be used. The foundation remains permanently behind the strings. Lightweight paper, thin, noniron interfacing, or tearaway stabilizer can also be used. These are torn away after sewing. For a nonfabric foundation, use a short stitch length on the sewing machine.

3 Mark the foundation with the shape you wish to cover. It should be larger than the template so that it accommodates take-up during sewing.

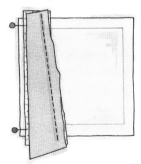

4 Place one string on the foundation right side up, aligning the raw edge with that of the foundation. The string should extend beyond the drawn shape at both ends. Pin to hold. Place a second string on top of the first, aligning raw edges and right side down. Pin, then stitch through all three layers, using a ¼-inch seam.

**Left:** Detail of *String Stars*, American, nineteenth century.

5 Grade the seam allowance to reduce the bulk, then open the second strip and press.

6 Continue to add strings until the foundation shape is covered. Press the pieced fabric.

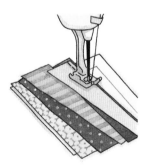

7 Place your template right side up on the right side of the pieced fabric. Draw around it with a fabric marker, then cut out the shape carefully. If using a paper foundation, remove it after cutting.

# CURVED PIECING

This Double Wedding Ring design presents two challenges: one is the accurate piecing needed for the arcs of the rings, and the second is the successful working of the curved seams required for assembling it. Machine paper-foundation piecing is the key to the first, while easing, the fitting together of two apparently opposing curves, answers the second. The instructions below will help with assembling any curved-seam design, such as Fans, Snail Trail or New York Beauty. You will notice a difference when sewing curves—the tracing paper is on top and the fabric is underneath.

## Making a Sample Block

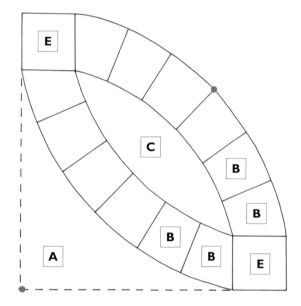

❶ Enlarge the above pattern of a D unit to 7½ inches between the red dots, to make templates for the background pieces A and C, adding a ¼-inch seam on all sides. Make eight tracings of the B ring unit. The solid line indicates the stitch line. Add a ¼-inch seam on all sides.

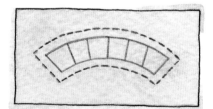

B unit

❷ To piece the B units, cut 2½-inch-wide strips from different-colored scrap fabrics.

❸ Place unit B foundation paper drawn side down. Center the first fabric strip, right side up, over one end and trim to a rough rectangle. Pin or hold in position with a dab of fabric glue.

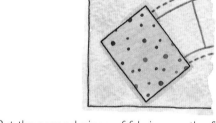

❹ Put the second piece of fabric over the first, right sides together, and pin to hold in place.

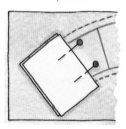

❺ Turn the work over so that the paper tracing is on top. Sew along the drawn stitching line into the seam allowances at the beginning and end.

**6** Turn the tracing fabric side up. Trim seam allowance to ¼ inch. Flip the second piece right side up and finger-press in place. Pin or hold with a dab of glue. Repeat until the tracing is covered with fabric. Make seven more units in the same way. Press and trim both the fabric and the tracing to the marked seam allowance.

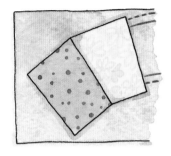

**7** Cut one A and four C patterns from the background fabric. Cut eight corner squares (E), four from light fabrics and four from dark fabrics, each 2 x 2 inches.

## Easing curved seams

**8** Put a pieced B unit with a C piece right sides together. With raw edges level, match the center and the ends. Carefully pin together at right angles to the sewing line, easing the fullness equally in the spaces between the pins. The pins should be inserted exactly ¼ inch from the raw edges. This is your sewing line.

**9** With the B unit on top, sew the two units together. Fold right sides over and press carefully. Repeat to make four more units.

## To Complete the Block

**10** Add a dark E square to both ends of two B units and a light E square to each end of the remaining two units.

**11** Sew one of these units to the strip completed in steps 3–7 to make four elliptical D units. Ease the curves together just as before, now also matching the corner of the E squares to the junction of the C piece and the B unit. Press.

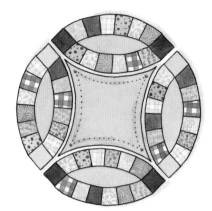

The finished block with one A unit
and four D units

**12** Mark the ¼-inch seam with a pencil dot on the wrong side of the A pieces at the four points. Do not sew beyond the dot.

**13** Place the A piece right side up and fit the D units with light E squares on top and bottom and the other D units to each side. Sew each ellipse to piece A. Remove the tracings from the B units once stitched in place.

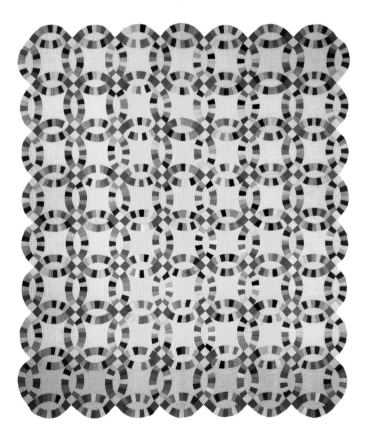

**Above:** *Double Wedding Ring,* American, nineteenth century.

**Above:** *Little Seaside Town*, wall hanging by Katharine Guerrier,
English, twentieth century.

# MINIATURE PATCHWORK

Manipulating small fabric pieces, whether cutting or sewing, presents even experienced quilters with difficulties. Stitching over a foundation marked with design lines achieves accurate results quickly, as the pieces are trimmed after sewing. Use a machine straight stitch over a paper foundation and then tear away the paper or use a muslin base and sew by hand or machine. The muslin remains behind the block and acts as a stabilizer. To be consistent, all border areas should be backed with the same weight of muslin.

## Making a Sample Tree Block

❶ Onto paper, accurately trace your design lines with a well-sharpened embroidery transfer crayon (fig. 1).

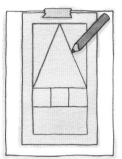

**fig. 1**                    **fig. 2**

❷ Place the tracing face down in the center of the foundation. Use a hot iron to transfer the design to the fabric (fig. 2). Several prints can be made from one tracing.

❸ Each shape on the template is numbered, and the pieces must be sewn in numerical order. For the trunk, select an appropriately colored scrap of fabric at least ¼ inch larger all around than the trunk shape. Place the scrap right side up on the unmarked side of the foundation. Hold the block up to the light to help position the fabric correctly. Pin and baste in place.

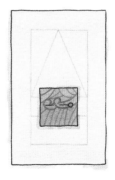

❹ For piece 2, cut a scrap of sky slightly larger than the template and position it right side down on top of the trunk. Align the raw edges, then pin and baste in position.

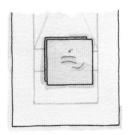

❺ Flip the block over to the printed side. Sew on the printed line, joining piece 1 to piece 2: start and finish stitching just beyond the ends of the printed lines. If machine sewing, choose a shorter stitch length (15 per inch) than for usual piecing.

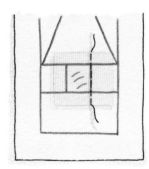

❻ Turn the block over and trim away the excess seam allowance. Press the pieces flat. Continue to trim and press after each step.

❼ In the same way, attach a second scrap of sky fabric to the opposite side of the trunk. Continue adding pieces in the sequence marked on the template. Ensure that all the pieces on the outer edges of the block are large enough for a ¼-inch seam allowance around the outside.

# CRAZY PATCHWORK

Crazy patchwork peaked in popularity in the latter half of the nineteenth century. The name refers to the irregular and random manner in which these quilts are pieced. Traditional crazy quilts often feature recognizable patchwork blocks, such as Log Cabin or Fans, as if included as practice pieces. Worked over a foundation fabric, crazy quilts are scrap quilts in origin; they are traditionally made with scraps of exotic fabrics like velvet, silk, and brocade. By nature, bright, colorful, and lavish crazy quilts are embellished with ribbons, lace, "found" objects, beads, small pictures, and embroidery. Shisha mirrors and sequins are modern additions.

The accompanying quilt project on page 106, inspired by the church of St. Eustache in Les Halles, Paris, is a modern interpretation of crazy patchwork and, unusually for this type of patchwork, contains batting. The quilt is worked as twenty-five separate units that are applied to a black background.

## Making a Sample Block

❶ Assemble a wide selection of textured fabric scraps, such as velvets, silks, and brocades. Collect an assortment of hand embroidery threads and objects to embellish the quilt surface, such as shisha mirrors, beads, and ribbons.

❷ Cut a foundation square of muslin larger all around than the finished project to allow for take-up.

❸ Begin in the center working outward (fig. 1), or at the corner and work across the foundation block (fig. 2). Position strips of fabric right side up and overlap by ½ inch. Pin in place. Work with the shapes as they are and trim the excess.

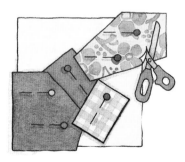 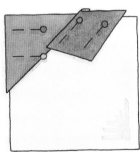

| fig. 1 | fig. 2 |

**Left:** Detail of *Crazy Quilt*, loaned by Brian Smith, English, early twentieth century.

❹ Turn under ¼ inch along the overlapped edges and blind-hem in position. Either work a piece at a time or position a few pieces, turning them under and basting as necessary, then blind-hem the group.

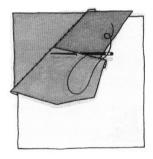

❺ When the foundation square is covered with patches, work decorative embroidery stitches over the seams. Embroider additional motifs as desired.

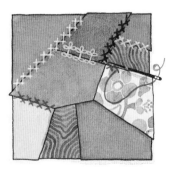

### TIPS
- Crazy borders for quilts can be assembled in the same way as the crazy quilt top by adding assorted patches to long foundation strips.

# chatelet **made by Gisela Thwaites**

## MATERIALS
- Batting 85 x 85 in. minimum (charcoal color if possible)
- 7½ yd. black
- 2 yd. muslin for foundation
- 2½ yd. approximately of mixed rich fabric scraps, such as silks, satins, brocades, and metallics
- 1 oz. purple chunky chenille yarn
- Assorted hand-embroidery threads
- Assorted embellishments, such as beads, sequins, and shisha mirrors
- Black machine and quilting thread

**Finished size** 62 x 62 in.

## CUTTING
- Make templates of the window shapes (see page 175). Make a full-size paper template of the whole design and cut out the window shapes.
- From calico, cut 12 squares, each 11½ in., for the hearts; 12 rectangles, 12½ x 6 in., for the wedges and one square, 12 in., for the circle. Mark a heart template in each 11½-in. square. Repeat for wedges and circle.
- Divide the black fabric into two lengths, each 66 in. long, and two lengths 68 in. long. Place each pair right sides together and sew along the selvage, using a ¾-in. seam. Trim away the selvage and press the seam open. The smaller piece is for the quilt top (center the seam horizontally), and the larger piece is for the backing (center the seam vertically).

**Above:** Detail of embellishment.

**Above:** Detail of embroidery.

## Sewing

1 Fill each shape with crazy patchwork. All the shapes incorporate light- and pale-colored fabrics to resemble a stained-glass window. Extend the patchwork filling ¼ in. beyond the outline of each shape. Replace the template to ensure that the whole area has been filled in, as the foundation can become distorted during sewing. Add any embroidery or other embellishments at this stage while the shapes are small enough to handle with ease.

2 Trim the foundation to include ¼-in. turnings. Turn under and baste the seam allowance.

3 Center the full-size paper pattern on the right side of the black fabric and mark the window positions through the cut-out shapes.

4 Position each of the crazy-pieced shapes on each marked window. Pin, baste, then blind-hem in position. Couch purple chenille yarn around the outline of each shape.

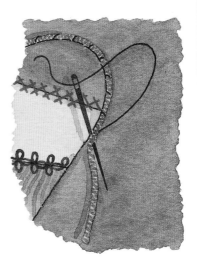

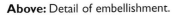

## Finishing

1 Assemble the three quilt layers (see page 47). Outline-quilt the window shapes. Fill the rest of the top with radiating lines of quilting.

2 Trim the quilt top to measure 62 x 62 in., ensuring the corners are square. Trim the batting to the same size. Trim the backing to be 1 in. larger on all sides. Fold the backing over to the front. Turn under ¼ in. around the raw edge of the backing and blind-hem in position. Add a hanging sleeve. Sign and date to finish.

**Above:** Detail of *Grandmother's Flower Garden*, American, early nineteenth century.

# HEXAGONS

This method, although old, is still an accurate way to hand piece tessellating designs. Hexagonal, or honeycomb, designs are traditionally worked over paper or cardboard templates that are removed as the units are sewn together.

Fabric hexagons are cut ¼ inch larger all around than the paper template, and the excess fabric is folded over the template and basted to secure. The basting is worked through all the layers, including the template.

The equal-sided hexagon is the most popular shape and appears in countless versions of Grandmother's Flower Garden. Elongated variations, such as the Church Window and the Coffin shape, appear in nineteenth-century English quilts and bedcovers.

Today, paper templates are sometimes replaced by a lining of interfacing. Iron-on interfacing stays in the finished work.

## Piecing Hexagons Over Papers

❶ Use the pattern below to make a master template without seam allowances from plastic, and use this to cut one template from stiff paper for each hexagon (old greeting cards are ideal).

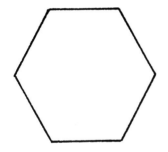

❷ Place the template on the wrong side of the fabric. Mark and cut a fabric hexagon with a ¼-inch seam allowance all around.

❸ Fold the seam allowance over the template, finger-press, and baste in place as shown. Prepare all hexagons in this way. For speed and greater ease, small pieces of masking tape can be used to hold the seam allowances in place.

## Joining Hexagons

❶ To join two hexagons, place right sides together with all sides even. Choose a sewing thread that blends with all the fabrics being stitched and whipstitch just into the edge of the fabrics where they are folded over the papers without catching the template. Make your stitches small and even. Secure the thread at the end with a couple of stitches.

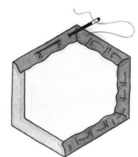

❷ Where possible, move onto an adjacent seam, picking up the next hexagon and holding it in place, right sides together, against an already stitched hexagon.

❸ Remove the basting threads and the templates after sewing together several hexagons. For support, keep the papers in place along the outside edges. Remove them on completion of the project.

# CATHEDRAL WINDOWS

Cathedral Windows projects are not true quilts in that they usually have no filling, but they are one of a group of novelty techniques that have been identified more closely with quilting than with any other sewing discipline.

The technique involves folding and refolding squares and stitching each together to give the appearance of windows. It is a deceptively simple technique and can be readily enjoyed by a needlework novice—a large square is folded to frame a smaller, contrasting-color square, and can be sewn successfully by hand.

## Making a Sample Window

**1** Cut two squares, each 6½ inches, of background fabric. Cut one 2-inch square of accent fabric for the window.

**2** Lightly mark the center of a 6½-inch square by folding along both diagonals and creasing lightly with the point of the iron. Turn under ¼ inch on all sides to the wrong side.

**3** Fold each corner into the center to make a block, 4⅛ inches. Using a needle and knotted thread, secure the corners in the center with a small cross-stitch. Do not cut the thread.

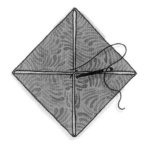

**4** Press, then fold the corners in again to the center point, press, and secure with a cross-stitch. The side with

the folds is the right side of the square. Repeat steps 2–4 for the second 6½-inch square.

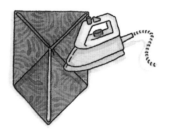

**5** Place two prepared squares right sides together and overcast invisibly along one edge. Do not stitch too tightly, as this makes a ridge preventing the pieces from lying flat.

**6** Place a 2-inch square on-point over this and pin. Trim until ⅛ inch of background is visible all around.

**7** Turn the bias folds of the background over the edges of the window square and stitch in place, stretching them into a smooth curve as you go. Blind-hem or use a tiny spaced backstitch. Do not stitch too tightly—a pinched look spoils the fine appearance.

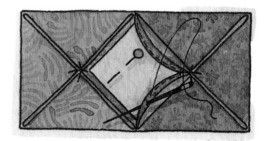

**8** At the corners, bring the two folds together, with a tiny bar-stitch about ¼ inch from the point ensuring that the raw edges of the window fabric underneath are covered.

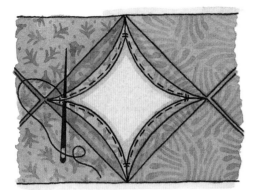

Bar stitch

# Secret Garden Unit

This simple-to-sew unit makes four neat petals. Combine it with the basic unit for more variety and flexibility of design.

**1** Cut one square, 6½ in., for the background and one window square, 3 in.

**2** Prepare the background square following the instructions in steps 2 and 3 on page 110. Cut the thread.

**3** Fold the four corners to the center again and press but do not stitch. Open out and check that the fold lines are clearly visible. If not, refold. Center the accent square on-point inside the folds. Trim if required. Secure the square with a small permanent running stitch close to the raw edges.

**4** Refold the corners to the center. Press and secure in the center with a cross-stitch.

**5** Turn the pairs of bias folds away from each other to reveal the accent fabric beneath and sew neatly in place.

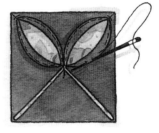

**6** Make a bar stitch to hold the folds together ¼ in. from the corner (see drawing at top of first column). Repeat with all four pairs of folds to make the four petals.

**7** To add greater variety and color to your Secret Garden units, make several different pieced four-patch accent squares.

**Left:** Detail of cathedral window and secret garden units, by Elizabeth Snodgrass, late twentieth century.

**Above:** *Schoolhouse Quilt,* by Annlee Landman, English, twentieth century. For instructions on how to make this quilt, see page114.

# REPRESENTATIONAL PATCHWORK

Pieced blocks are most commonly associated with abstract geometric patterns. However, there are a number of representational designs that remain firm favorites with quilters. These include Maple Leaf, variations of the Pine Tree design, Sailboat, and numerous Basket designs. Many subjects can be simplified into basic geometric components, and with a skillful combination of straight lines and curved piecing, new designs can be created.

There are no hard-and-fast rules of representing objects in patchwork, because much depends on the quilter's skill in translating the design into a workable unit, and the amount of detail needed for a realistic representation. Successful patterns are those that translate easily into geometric shapes. The accompanying project on page 114 uses a variation of the popular Schoolhouse design.

## Designing a Representational Block

① Choose an image for your representational block. Use two L-shaped framing strips made of cardboard to help identify the parts of the image you want to use.

② Place tracing paper over the image and trace the main shapes. Curves can be drawn in freehand at this stage.

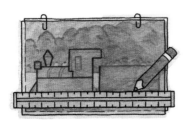

③ From the tracing, decide on the most suitable block shape for the motif, such as square or square on-point.

④ Draw the block outline on to graph paper. Transfer the image, maintaining the proportions of the parts into the block outline. Tidy freehand drawn curves with a compass.

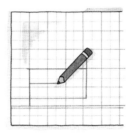

⑤ Study the design to determine how to sew it most efficiently. Look for awkward inset corners or very sharp angles. If necessary, continue existing seams to the edge of the block. Then use fabric pattern or color to conceal these essential construction lines. Consider using the method for miniature patchwork blocks on page 103.

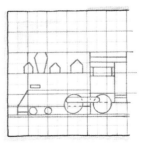

⑥ Return to your original picture to identify which remaining details are needed to complete the representation effectively. Shapes that are too awkward for piecing may be appliquéd or embroidered.

⑦ Make a paper pattern and sew a test block from scrap fabrics. When the block is successful, ink in the pattern with a fine-line marker to make the master design.

# schoolhouse quilt

### made by Annelee Landman

## MATERIALS

- 1½ yd. backing and sleeve
- 1¼ yd. 60-in.-wide batting
- ½ yd. unbleached muslin
- Scraps at least 3 x 19 in. each, of 12 different plaids
- ⅝ yd. navy for setting strips
- Scraps, minimum 5 x 10 in., of garnet red, ginger, and earthy red for sashing squares
- ¼ yd. yellow for outer border
- ¼ yd. red plaid for binding
- Matching sewing thread and embroidery threads for tying

**Finished size** 36 x 47 in.
**Block size** 9 x 9 in.
**Number of blocks** 12

## CUTTING
### NAVY

- Cut eight strips, each 2½ in. wide, across the width of the fabric. From these, cut 31 strips, each 9½ in. long.

### YELLOW

- Cut five strips, 1 in. wide, across the width of the fabric. From two of these, cut strips 38 in. long for top and bottom outer borders. Divide a third strip in half. Trim the selvages from the two remaining strips, then to each strip add half of the third strip. Trim to 48 in. long for side outer borders.

### RED PLAID

- Cut strips 1½ in. wide across the width of the cloth and 176 in. long in total for ¼-in. double binding.

### SASHING SQUARES

- Cut scraps into 2½-in. wide strips, then cross-cut into a total of 20 squares, each 2½ in., in a mixture of colors.

## UNBLEACHED MUSLIN

- Cut 10 strips, each 1½ in. wide, across the width of the fabric. From these, cut 12 strips 19 in. long (A, B, C, D); 12 strips 6½ in. (M); 12 strips 3½ in. (O), and 24 strips 2 in. long (F).
- Cut 12 rectangles, each 2¼ x 3 in. To make triangles for the roof section, divide six rectangles diagonally top left to bottom right—this will make 12 for the right-hand end of the block J. Divide the remaining six from bottom left to top right to make 12 triangles for the left-hand end (K).
- Cut 12 strips, each 1¼ x 5 in. (I), to divide the roof gable from the side.

## EACH SCHOOLHOUSE PLAID

- Cut two strips, each 1½ x 19 in. (A, B, C, D). Divide one strip into lengths of 10 in. (C, D), 5½ in. (G), and 3½ in. (E).
- Cut a rectangle 2½ x 7½ in. for the side of the roof (H). Mark 2 in. from the lower left-hand corner along the bottom and from the top right-hand corner along the top. Cut from the appropriate corner to the mark to make the required parallelogram.
- Cut a rectangle 2⅝ x 4 in. (L). Mark the midpoint of one long side. With a rotary cutter and a ruler, cut from opposite corners to the midpoint mark to make the roof gable.
- Cut two pieces, each 1½ x 2 in., for the chimneys (N).

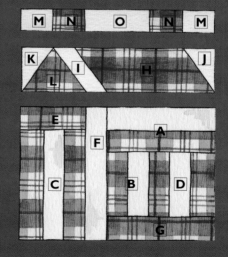

## Making One Schoolhouse Block

1 With right sides together, sew the 19-in. plaid to a matching muslin. Press seam toward plaid. Cut one 5½-in. length for the top of window (A) and one 3½-in. for the vertical (B).

2 To the muslin side of the remaining strip add the 10-in. plaid. Cut one 5½-in. strip (C) and one 3½-in. (D).

3 To one short side of the C piece, sew a plaid 3½-in. strip (E) to make the top of the doorway. Press open, then add a muslin strip 6½ in. (F) long to the right-hand side.

 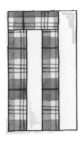 

4 Sew pieced units B and D together, keeping the sequence correct for the window. Sew a plaid 5½-in. strip (G) to the lower edge. Press, then add the A unit to the top.

5 Sew the window unit to the right-hand side of the door unit.

6 Pin the 1¼-in.-wide muslin strip (I) on one of the short parallelogram (H) sides and sew. After pressing, trim the excess muslin level top and bottom.

7 Sew triangle J to the other end, positioning it carefully with ¼-in. points extended beyond the roof edge.

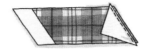 

8 Stitch the remaining muslin triangle K to the left side of the roof gable (L). Press, then sew the gable to the roof side.

9 Alternate the remaining 1½-in.-wide strips of muslin (M) and plaid (N) at each side of the muslin 3½-in. strip (O) and seam together. Assemble the chimney, roof, and house together.

## Finishing

1 Make 11 more schoolhouse blocks. Arrange the blocks into four rows of three blocks. Sew the rows of blocks together with navy setting strips.

2 Sew five horizontal setting units by alternating four contrast sashing squares and three navy strips. Join the rows of blocks and setting units.

3 Attach a long yellow outer border to the two sides of the quilt, trimming as necessary. Add the remaining yellow strips to the top and bottom, trimming accordingly.

4 Layer the quilt (see page 47), and in the center of the blocks and sashing squares, use three colors of embroidery thread to tie the quilt, trimming tails to approximately ½ in. (see page 173).

5 Finish with ¼-in. red plaid binding (see page 52). Add a sleeve for hanging (see page 57). Sign and date your quilt to finish.

**Above:** *Color-wash Stripes with White Triangles*, by Deirdre Amsden, English, twentieth century.

# COLOR-WASH PATCHWORK

Color-wash patchwork refers to the technique of piecing together small squares of printed fabric to create shaded abstract designs. The technique is influenced by the impressionist paintings in which colors and values change almost imperceptibly across the surface of the work. The impression of form is created by the pattern size and subtle blend of colors. A concentration of color at the center of the design, diffusing outward and emphasized by patterns of increasing size, creates depth and proportion. When selecting fabrics, avoid ginghams, stripes, and polka dots (mini-dots may be suitable), as these designs are often too distinctive to blend together satisfactorily.

## Practicing the Color-wash Technique

1 Choose a wide range of printed fabrics in varying colors, hues, and pattern sizes. From each, cut squares of 2 or 3 inches. Smaller squares may not offer enough of a pattern, while larger squares may provide too much of one color or pattern, so that it dominates. Use the wrong side of a print fabric to yield a softer shade.

2 Sort the squares by color, then by tonal value (light, medium, and dark) within each color family. Use the color wheel to help blend the colors. To help sort out the color values, put anything not read instantly as light or dark into the medium pile. Divide the medium selection again into medium-light and medium-dark.

3 Next, choose swatches from two color ranges. Arrange one set of squares in a column from dark to light and the

Light      Medium      Dark

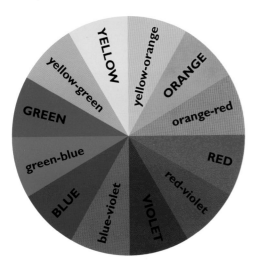

second set from light to dark, blending the two together in the center so that the medium colors diffuse into each other. Repeat the same exercise using just one color and differing values. The aim is to create a unit block in which the fabric swatches all blend with each other without jarring or drawing attention to any one square. Be prepared to discard any squares that prove too eye-catching. Finally, arrange blocks of different colors or values to create contrasts between blocks.

4 A reducing glass identifies any errors in position, but using the viewfinder of a camera or the wrong end of a pair of binoculars works equally well. Look through red cellophane or a red plastic viewer to more easily detect errors in value placement of your fabric selection.

# vase of flowers

**made by Jill Cawrey**

## MATERIALS
- 1 yd. backing
- 1 yd. batting
- ¼ yd. turquoise for binding
- ½ yd. random-dyed turquoise for inner and outer borders and vase
- ½ yd. peach print for first background and middle border
- ¼ yd. peach-cream print for second background
- ¼ yd. peach-turquoise for the tablecloth
- Scraps of three prints showing sprigs of flowers for the outer sprays of flowers on light peach or cream grounds
- Scraps of seven densely packed small floral prints, each with different background colors
- Cream sewing thread
- Peach and light turquoise quilting thread

**Finished size 32 x 28 in.**

## CUTTING
### RANDOM-DYED TURQUOISE
- For the inner border, cut two strips 1 x 28 in. and two 1 x 24 in. For the outer border, cut two strips 2½ x 34 in. and two 2½ x 30 in.
- For the vase, cut a 2-in.-wide strip from the width of the fabric, and cross-cut into 14 squares, each 2 in.

### TURQUOISE BINDING
- Cut strips 1 in. wide totaling 135 in. for the binding to finish ¼ in.

### PEACH
- For the middle border, cut two strips, each 2 x 30 in., and two strips each 2 x 26 in.

### PEACH AND PEACH-CREAM BACKGROUND PRINTS
- From both fabrics, cut strips 2 in. wide and cross-cut into 2-in. squares, to yield a total of 86 squares, (not necessarily equal numbers of each print).

### PEACH-TURQUOISE PRINT
- For the tablecloth cut strips 2 in. wide and cross-cut into 28 squares, each 2 in.

### OUTER FLORAL SPRAYS
- Cut 29 squares, each 2 in., focusing on the printed sprigs.

### FLORAL PRINTS
- Cut 81 squares, each 2 in., from the seven different prints. Use the chart on the next page as a guide.

## KEY FOR COLOR-WASH

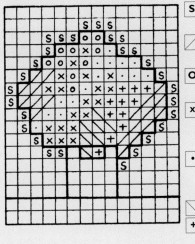

| | |
|---|---|
| **S** | Floral prints on cream grounds |
| ◹ | Blue/turquoise ground and flowers |
| **O** | Red ground and blue/mauve flowers |
| **x** | Red ground, red/orange/turquoise flowers |
| **·** | Smallest flowers brown, cream, orange, turquoise |
| ◺ | Magenta ground |
| **+** | Dark blue ground, red flowers |

## Sewing

1 Arrange the 28 peach-turquoise squares for the tablecloth.

2 Assemble the vase. Use the back of some of the squares to suggest a lighter side of the vase.

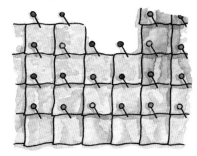

3 Fill in the background squares, arranging the two fabrics in a checkerboard design.

4 Use the chart as a guide to position each of the flower sprays. The final arrangement will depend on the choice of fabrics. The deeper colors were placed low in the arrangement, and the fabric with the smallest flowers was sprinkled diagonally across, creating an illusion of airiness and light. Stand back and review the composition. Be prepared to rearrange squares and discard some. Use the back of the fabric to aid transition from one area to another.

5 Sew the squares together in rows, using ¼-in. seam allowances. Press the turnings in opposite directions on adjacent rows before sewing the rows together to complete the center panel. This will ensure that the seams interlock (see page 37).

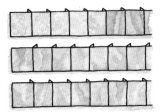

6 To assemble the border strips into four sets, first find the centers of all strips. Match the centers of adjacent strips when sewing the peach middle border between the two turquoise strips, again with ¼-in. seams, so that the sets will already be shorter on the inside ends for the miters.

7 To attach the borders, match the midpoint of the sides of the center panel to the midpoints of the borders and sew accurately ¼ in. from the end at both start and finish on each side. Fold and sew the miters as directed on page 42.

## Finishing

1 The flowers were quilted with a petal-like design similar to the traditional wineglass pattern. This should be marked on the quilt top in the flower spray only.

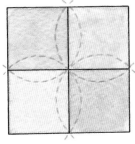

2 Assemble the quilt layers (see page 47), pin, and baste.

3 Work the marked quilting design. Add horizontal quilting lines across the tablecloth and diagonals across the background as if radiating outward from the center. Quilt in-the-ditch around the borders.

4 Prepare the edges with a row of permanent basting, then add ¼-in. binding with automatic miters (see page 50). Sign and date the quilt, then add a hanging sleeve to finish (see page 55).

**Above:** *Flower Power*, by Maria Reuter, German, twentieth century. For instructions on how to make this quilt, see page 122.

# FRAGMENTATION

Fragmentation refers to the division of patchwork blocks into smaller units. Adding more pieces to the design allows greater interplay of shape, color, and tone, creating a sense of movement and adding visual interest. For accurate construction, this technique demands competence in the piecing and assembling of basic units, an understanding of color, and a strong sense of design.

For the lesson, use the Four Card Trick block as the whole quilt top and fragment it using straight seams. Then consider ways to fragment the background. Fragmentation is most successful when the eye perceives an overall unity. Symmetrical designs need not always be fragmented in the same way throughout.

## Fragmenting a Block

1 On paper, draw the various components of the block; divide the blocks in the following way:

2 Subdivide the units in different ways. Experiment by leaving parts of the original design undivided or by fragmenting the whole unit.

3 Interpret these designs using fabric scraps or colored pencils. Experiment with color and hue, making subtle changes by altering the basic color by degrees of light and dark (fig. 1). For example, grade from the darkest shades in the center to lighter shades at the outer edges.

4 Alternatively, use contrasting colors to create a dramatic effect in the center of the unit (fig. 2). From these experiments, choose those fragmentations that work best together and color in the whole design (fig. 3).

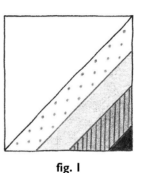

**fig. 1**

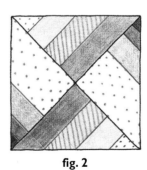

**fig. 2**

**fig. 3** Four Card Trick Block

# flower power quilt

**made by Maria Reuter**

**ADVANCED**

**Finished size** 78 x 78 in.
**Block size** 8 x 8 in.
**Number of blocks** 81

## MATERIALS

- 85 x 85 in. (minimum) batting
- 2¼ yd. 90-in.-wide backing
- 1¾ yd. black
- Mixed pastel prints on a light background equivalent to 2½ yd.
- Mixed colorful medium prints equivalent to 2½ yd.
- Mixed dark prints on a black background equivalent to 3½ yd.
- Graph paper
- Cardboard or template plastic

## CUTTING
## TEMPLATES

- Make 8-in. templates for patterns 1–4.

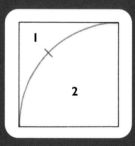
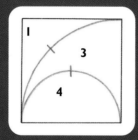

- On graph paper, draw two squares, each 8 in. In each square draw a grid of four rows of four squares. Divide each block into its component parts by drawing the curved lines on the grid. Cut out the shapes.

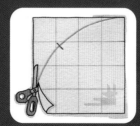

- To understand the piecing of each curve, attach each shape to a 8-in. square of cardboard and continue the grid squares on the cardboard to complete the squares. These grids show the configuration of pieces to be sewn, and on which the templates fit.

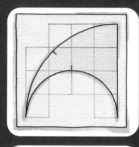

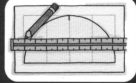

## BLACK

- From the width of the fabric, cut eight strips, 3½ in. wide, for the borders.
- From the width of the fabric, cut eight strips, 2 in. wide, joining them together to make continuous binding.
- Using template 1 and adding seam allowances, cut eight shapes; cut one shape using template 3; and cut three shapes using template 4.

## MIXED PRINTS, ALL VALUES

- Cut strips 2½ in. wide from all fabrics and cross-cut into 2½-in. squares. Separate the three values.

## KEY

| | |
|---|---|
| ■ Solid black | ▨ Medium prints |
| ▨ Dark prints | □ Pastel prints |

## Sewing

1 The quilt top is pieced together in nine sections of nine blocks each. This keeps the units manageable but of a scale sufficient to ensure that the colors of each block flow easily into the next. Use the key as a guide to the correct position of each tonal value.

2 For each configuration in turn, sew together pieces of the correct value. Press the seams.

3 Using the templates, cut each shape from the relevant pieced unit, adding seam allowances and marking center points.

4 Arrange nine blocks in each group. There should be a harmonious transition of color between blocks.

5 Sew the curved shapes together into single blocks, using a ¼-in. seam allowance, following the directions for curved seams (see page 87).

6 Sew the blocks into rows of three, then stitch the three rows together to complete each section.

7 To make sure that the colors of one section flow into or contrast with the next, keep completed sections together when arranging the color scheme of the remaining blocks. A design board would be useful here.

8 Stitch together the nine sections.

## Finishing

1 Join the border strips lengthwise, two for each side of the top. Then attach each border to the quilt top, using either straight-cut or mitered corners (see page 42).

2 Layer, pin, and baste the quilt top, batting, and backing. Protect the edges by folding over excess backing.

3 Hand quilt or machine quilt the design, following the curves of the motifs.

4 Add a line of permanent basting within the seam allowance around the edges. Trim the batting and backing ¼ in. larger than the quilt top.

5 Add the binding, sewing ½ in. from the trimmed edge. Fold over and blind-hem into place to finish ½ in. wide.

6 Sign and date your quilt (see page 55).

**Above:** *Cuilfail Spiral*, by Jan Hale,
English, twentieth century.
**Left:** *Ohio Star*, by Susan Chastney,
English, twentieth century.

# OPTICAL-ILLUSION PATCHWORK

From the mid-nineteenth century, optical-illusion quilts have developed into an art form. With no formal training in geometry or color, some quilters chose to make quilts that challenged the normal perceptions of a simple bedcover, creating quilts that artistically preceded their generation by at least a hundred years.

Optical-illusion quilts cause the eye to see a three-dimensional shape while the mind recognizes the flat surface of the quilt. By manipulating color, shape, and line, and by placing light and dark blocks in juxtaposition to each other, quilters create receding or advancing images, a sense of movement, increasing or decreasing space, and layers of design.

Traditional patterns, such as Tumbling Blocks, Log Cabin variations, and Kaleidoscope, give the illusion of three dimensions. With transparency, the mind sees layers of color that appear to pass in front of or behind each other. With vibration solid complementary or contrasting colors of the same value are placed side-by-side repeatedly to dazzle the eye, as in the Black-and-White quilt on page 126.

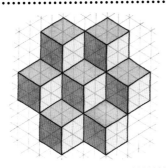

## Designing a Three-dimensional Grid

❶ On isometric graph paper, imagine a light shining at one corner of the paper. Using a light-value pencil, color in all the diamonds that face toward the light. The shapes on the opposite side, away from the imagined light, should be colored with a dark color. The remaining diamonds should be colored with a medium-value pencil.

## Transparency

❶ To demonstrate the effect of transparency, cut two triangles from different-colored transparent material, such as cellophane or chiffon. Overlay one triangle over the other at different angles. At the point of overlap, a third color appears (fig.1). This is transparency in its simplest form.

❷ The more difficult aspect of transparency is in the translation of illusion into pieced fabric. In the Ohio Star quilt opposite, one large Ohio Star block appears to float over a background of small Ohio Star blocks. The large star appears to stand independent of its background and, at the same time, to merge with it. The effect is created by the use of two predominant color schemes. Light and bright shades of pink and yellow are used in the large star, while hues of black, navy, and gray merge to form a dark background. The overall unity of the design is retained by the muted colors that cause the large star of the foreground to blend into the background. The large star design is a reflection of the smaller stars—this repetition draws the design together.

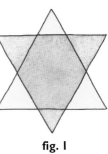

**fig. 1**

## Vibration

❶ This exercise is to understand how colors interact and make each other seem to vibrate. Using the color wheel on page 117, collect bright, solid-colored paper samples of the same value, choosing colors from all parts of the color spectrum. Choose one color and place it on top of the other colors in turn to study the effect. Maximum vibration occurs between identical values of two colors exactly opposite each other on the color wheel.

# black-and-white
## optical-illusion quilt

**made by Maria Reuter**

2½-in. units

## MATERIALS
- 2⅜ yd. 80-in.-wide backing
- 85 x 85 in. (minimum) batting
- 3¼ yd. black
- 2½ yd. total solid white and a variety of white-on-white (patterned) fabrics
- 1 yd. striped fabric for binding
- Matching sewing and quilting thread

**Finished size 78¾ x 72¾ in.**

## CUTTING
### BLACK
- Cut eight strips, each 5½ in. wide, across the width of the fabric and set aside for borders.
- Across the width of the fabric, cut strips 3 in. wide. Cut more as required.

### WHITE
- Across the width of the fabric, cut strips from the solid white 3 in. wide. Cut more as required.
- Cut strips of different widths from the white-on-white fabrics.

### STRIPED FABRIC
- Cut strips 4½ in. wide across the width of the fabric to total 8¾ yd. for binding, to finish 2 in. wide.

## Sewing

1 Following the instructions on page 79 for strip-piecing, stitch together the white-on-white lengths of fabric in a random manner. Press.

2 Using a quilter's ruler, mark a 45° angle across the direction of the strips. Parallel to the marked line, cut diagonal strips 3 in. wide. Make more as required to use for the shaded white-on-white areas. Use the plan on page 188 as a placement guide.

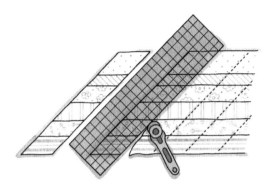

3 Above the quilt opposite is a scale, each unit measuring 2½ in. Where a strip changes color diagonally, that unit must be added to both colors (see below). To calculate the length of each section, count the number of units (counting twice at diagonals). Multiply this figure by 2½ in., then add ½ in. for seams.

4 For example, for the left-hand side of the top strip, cut two 3 in. squares from the 3-in.-wide black strips, and one 20½ in. strip. From solid white, cut two 8-in. strips. Arrange each in the correct sequence.

5 Stitch one horizontal strip at a time. The sections are joined at a 45° angle, as for continuous binding. Finger-press a diagonal on one black square. Place with the 8-in. white strip, right sides together, aligning short raw edges. Pin, then stitch across the diagonal fold, making sure the seam slopes in the correct direction (fig. 1). Trim away the excess fabric and press (fig. 2). Place the second black strip at the other end of the white strip, right sides together and at a right angle to it. Stitch across the diagonal (fig. 3).

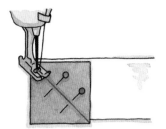

fig. 1

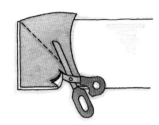

fig. 2

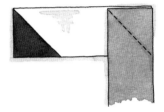

fig. 3

6 Continue to stitch one strip at a time, including the patterned strip-pieced whites. Check all strips following the quilt plan before joining each together to complete the top.

## Finishing

1 Join the 5½-in.-wide strips as necessary to make the borders. Sew to the sides, top, and bottom of the quilt.

2 Layer, pin, and baste. Echo-quilt inside the squares and triangles fabric at 2-in. intervals. Quilt remaining background with a single line along the middle of the strip.

3 Prepare the edges with a row of permanent basting just inside the ¼-in. turning. Trim the edges of the backing and batting to 1¾ in. larger than the quilt top.

4 Join the striped binding and attach to the quilt with a ¼-in. seam. Fold over to the back, turn in ¼ in., and sew to the machine stitching, to finish 2 in. wide.

# APPLIQUÉ TECHNIQUES

Appliqué is simply a technique of stitching fabric shapes onto a background to create a design. It can also be used to repair damaged or worn clothing. Its appeal lies in the infinite variety of possible designs. The technique dates back to the ancient Egyptians and examples can be found in early European and Asian needlework. During the medieval period, appliqué was used to decorate clothing, military banners, ecclesiastical robes, bed hangings, and household furniture.

Appliqué is often considered a more luxurious associate of patchwork. The appliqué quilt was once thought to be a "best quilt," to be brought out only on special occasions. As a result, appliqué quilts have fared better than their utilitarian counterparts, and many magnificent examples survive as a testament to the skill and artistry of nineteenth century needlewomen.

Appliqué has many forms, including Broderie perse, Hawaiian appliqué, and Mola appliqué. Most can be applied either by hand, invisibly or decoratively, by machine with an invisible blind-hem stitch, or by decorative machine embroidery stitches, such as satin stitch. It is an expressive technique that allows much freedom in design and execution.

**Left:** Detail of *Love Apple*, American, early nineteenth century.

# LIBRARY OF APPLIQUÉ BLOCKS

Although the pictorial nature of appliqué invites any motif as a suitable subject, the most popular motif traditionally has been the flower. In the nineteenth century, during the heyday of fine appliqué quilts, flowers appear in bouquets, wreaths, sprays, urns, baskets, vases, and garlands, and as single blooms. The ubiquitous rose appears in numerous guises—from the biblical *Rose of Sharon*, to the political *Whig Rose*.

During the appliqué revival of the 1920s, the market was flooded with new commercial designs that often reflected the popular culture of the time, such as Sunbonnet Sue, Bronco Buster, Colonial Lady, and a variety of figures from nursery rhymes. Still, despite the pictorial innovation in available patterns, floral designs continue to be the most popular subject for appliqué design.

Frequently seen combinations of hearts, birds, and potted flowers reflect a strong link to folk-art motifs from the areas known today as southern Germany, Austria, and Switzerland, and it is not too fanciful to imagine a link between their folded paper-cut designs and the appliqué designs used by the Pennsylvania Dutch quilters. The four-way and eight-way symmetry of folded-paper designs are a feature of nineteenth-century appliqué.

Many nineteenth-century appliqué quilts share a color scheme of red and green on a light background. Artistically complementary, these colors were chosen as a result of contemporary conditions—plain muslin as a background was cheap and plentiful, most vegetable dyes were unstable, and Turkey Red cloth, although expensive, was reliably colorfast and brilliant in hue.

The appliqué designs below and on the following page are just a starting point. In the tradition of the art, modify a design to please your taste or better still, make up your own, using simplified forms of motifs with personal significance.

Cockscomb and Currant

Cornucopia

Pinecone

Whig Rose

Fleur-de-lis

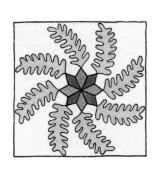

Princess Feather

Berries

Rose Wreath

Love Apple

Patriotic Eagle

Tulip Basket

Iris

Sunbonnet Sue

Farmer Bill

Scottie Dog

Snowflake

Oak Leaf and Reel

Bluebird

# HAND APPLIQUÉ FIRST STEPS

Good preparation is essential to speedy and accurate appliqué. Preparation need not be limited to one method, as no one of them gives more accurate results; try all methods and use those that work best for you. Finger-pressing is fast if you choose to appliqué using the needle-turning technique. Basting shapes before applying them allows for maximum control when sewing down. Card-pressing with starch is good for bold simple motifs, and the shapes can be applied to the background with any hand stitch. Using freezer paper for appliqué preparation ensures a stable and crisp edge when sewing.

## Enlarging a Design

The easiest way to enlarge any appliqué design is with a photocopier. However, you may prefer to enlarge the design using the grid method.

❶ Make an exact drawing of the size of block you intend to use and mark with a grid of equal-size squares, each no larger than 2 in. (fig. 1).

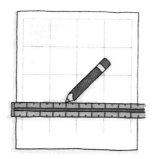

**fig. 1**

❷ Draw a grid of the same number of squares over the design you wish to enlarge (fig. 2).

**fig. 2**

❸ Copy each part of the original design onto the corresponding square of the large grid (fig. 3).

**fig. 3**

## Preparing the Background Fabric

❶ Cut blocks 1 inch larger to allow for take-up. The background can become distorted during sewing, particularly with elaborate designs.

❷ Finger-press vertical and horizontal center lines on the background for ease of positioning the design. For on-point designs, lightly crease the diagonals.

❸ Mark positioning lines only; do not draw the whole design. This is time-consuming, and it can be difficult to remove markings if the appliqué drifts slightly during sewing.

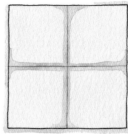

❹ Place the background over the master design and mark with a pencil your placement lines and points where two or more shapes overlap. Mark the linear shapes, such as basket handles, leaves, and stems, with a broken center line.

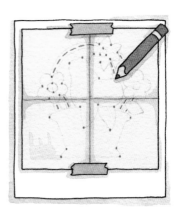

## Marking and Cutting Motifs

Whenever practical, match the grain of the appliqué motif with the grain of the background fabric. This prevents motifs from puckering.

**2** Cut out the shapes, adding a ¼-inch seam allowance by eye.

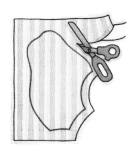

### Working with light-colored fabrics

**1** Tape the design right side up on a backlit surface, such as a light box or a window, then place the fabric right side up over it. With a well-sharpened pencil, trace the outline of the shape. The tracing line is your fold-under line. Leave a ½-inch space between outlines to allow for turnings.

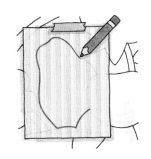

### Working with dark-colored fabrics

For dark fabrics, make a template without seam allowances. Use it to mark the outline of each shape on the right side of the fabric with either a light-colored pencil or a sharpened sliver of soap. Cut out carefully, adding a ¼-inch seam allowance by eye.

Templates are not necessary for straight shapes, such as stems. Cut straight strips on the straight grain and press or baste the turnings in place. Curved stems must be cut on the bias, then pressed and/or basted (see page 135).

## Preparation for Sewing

### Card-pressing with starch

**1** Using cardboard, make a pressing template without seam allowances for the heart.

**2** Protect the ironing board with a pressing cloth. Place heart right side down on the protected surface and center the pressing template over it.

**3** Spray some starch into a container—the lid of the can will do. Dip a cotton swab into the liquid starch and paint it onto the seam allowance around the template.

**4** Using a dry iron set on "cotton," press the seam allowance over the template with just the point of the iron. Press until the starch is dry and holds the turned seam allowance in place. Work all around the shape, easing in the fullness on the curves as necessary. Fold the fabric into a neat point and press at the base of the heart. At the notch, clip into the angle just before pressing. Strengthen before clipping with a dab of liquid fray preventer. Apply liquid according to the manufacturer's directions only to the area to be clipped.

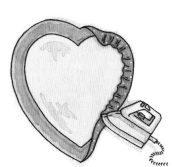

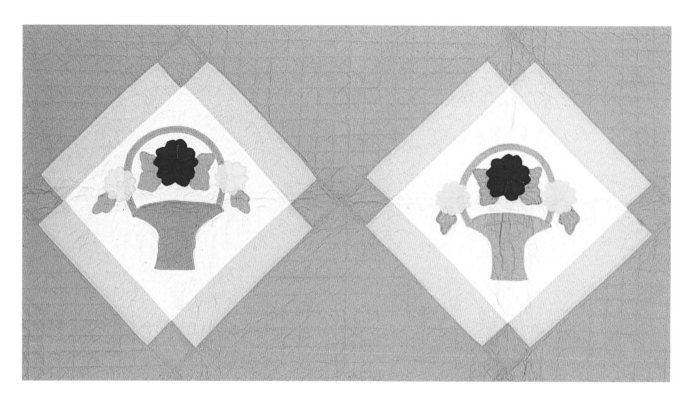

**Above:** Detail of *Flower Baskets*, American, ca. 1940.

## Finger-creasing

This is good preparation for needle-turned appliqué because the seam allowance turns under neatly along the creased line when stroked under with the point of your needle.

❶ Hold an appliqué shape right side up. Fold the turning along the drawn line away from you to the wrong side and pinch to form a crease. If you are creasing in the right place, you will not be able to see the pencil line. If you can see the line on the right side of the shape, the shape will be too big. Alternatively, if the pencil line is tucked under too far, your shape will be too small for the project.

❷ Don't run your fingers along as you crease or you will stretch the shape. Turn the shape as you work all the way around. Inside curves will not stay under without being snipped. Clip almost to the pencil line, but do not clip until actually sewing in place (see step 7 on page 138).

## Basting

Basting is useful for complex appliqué designs in which the pieces must fit together exactly to prevent gaps from appearing in the work.

❶ Hold the appliqué shape with the right side toward you. Fold the turning to the wrong side along the pencil line and baste in place with thread, leaving the beginning knot on the right side of the shape for easy removal later.

❷ Edges that will be covered by another appliqué need not be basted. If necessary, snip inside curves as you reach them and space the basting stitches to hold the turnings in place. A group of basted shapes can be correctly positioned on the background fabric, then either pinned or basted before sewing in place with your chosen stitch.

# Stitches for Hand Appliqué

## Running Stitch

Work the appliqué running stitch close to the turned-under edge of the shapes or ⅛ inch from raw-edge appliqué.

## Whipped Variation

To make the stitching decorative, whip the running stitches attaching the motif either with the same-color thread or with a contrast. This is a good way to emphasize the motif.

## Blind-hem Stitch

When you use this stitch, the motifs appear to be held invisibly. Hold the edge of the motif toward you. Always bring the thread out in the folded edge and never on the top of the motif. The stitches must be small, even, and close together to prevent the seam allowance from unfolding or frayed threads from appearing. Avoid pulling the sewing thread too tight as this creates a pinched appearance and puckers the block.

## Blanket and Buttonhole Stitches

Blanket and buttonhole stitches add definition around the outer edges of each motif. Blanket stitch can be worked in a fairly open manner on motifs with a turning pressed under and provides a decorative edging. The stitches of buttonhole stitching are worked close together to secure and protect cut edges, as in Broderie Perse. Fine, shaded embroidery thread is particularly effective for this appliqué technique.

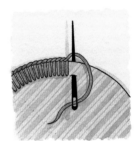

**Buttonhole Stitch**

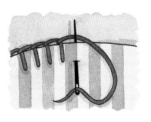

**Blanket Stitch**

**Long and Short Blanket Stitch**

## Preparing Stems

For straight stems and bias stems
Right side down, press fold along one edge.

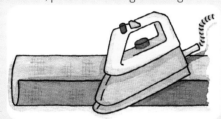

Press the second edge to almost reach the first fold.

Prepare bias strips in the same way for curved stems.

## Protecting Appliqué Shapes

Sharp notches within shapes need to be protected. Stabilize potential weak spots with a small dab of a liquid fray preventer applied to the turning. Allow to dry before sewing in place. Snip into the turning at the treated point; the fabric will not fray.

# tulips wall hanging
### made by Annlee Landman

**BEGINNER / INTERMEDIATE**

## CUTTING MUSLIN
- Cut a 24-in. backing square.
- Cut nine background squares for appliqué, each 6 in. These will be trimmed to the required 5½ in. after working the appliqué.

## GRAY-GREEN
- Cut two squares, each 8½ in., and divide on both diagonals to make eight side triangles.
- Cut two squares, each 5½ in., and divide once diagonally to make four corner setting triangles.
- Cut four 5½-in. setting squares.

## DEEP RED PRINT
- Cut straight-grain strips 1 in. wide and totaling 98 in. long for binding.

## SCRAPS OF RED AND RED PRINT
- Cut 27 B petals and 27 Br petals.
- Cut 27 A petals.

## DARK GREEN
- Cut nine straight-grain strips, each ¾ in. wide by 4½ in. long.
- Cut nine bias strips, each ¾ in. wide and 5 in. long, enough for two curved stems on one block.
- Cut 18 leaves.

## MATERIALS
- ¾ yd. muslin for backing
- ¾ yd. batting
- ½ yd. gray-green
- ½ yd. deep red print for binding
- Red and red print scraps for tulips
- Dark green scraps for stems and leaves

**Finished size** 21½ x 21½ in.
**Block size** 5 x 5 in.
**Number of appliqué blocks** 9

1 Work nine tulip blocks following the instructions on page 137.

2 Press the blocks face down over a hand towel (see page 37). Trim to 5½ x 5½ in.

3 Arrange the blocks on-point with the squares, side triangles, and corner triangles. Sew together in diagonal rows, pressing seams toward the gray-green where possible. Do not worry that the side triangles are oversized.

4 Using the tulip template, mark the four alternating squares. Use the tulip in the side triangles and the leaves in the corner triangles.

5 Assemble the quilt layers (see page 47) and baste. Work the quilting (see page 167).

6 Trim the quilt layers for a ¼-in. finished binding. Stitch permanent basting through all layers within the seam allowance. Follow the directions on page 50 to attach the continuous binding.

7 Make and attach a sleeve (see page 57). Sign and date your quilt to finish (see page 55).

# NEEDLE-TURNING TECHNIQUE

Needle-turning describes how the point of the needle strokes the seam allowance on the appliqué shape to turn it under immediately before sewing. Generally, the term is associated with appliqué that looks as if the stitching is invisible because it has been worked with a very neat and inconspicuous blind-hem stitch. It is possible to needle-turn the edges and sew with other stitches, such as running and buttonhole or blanket stitch.

## Making a Sample Tulip Block

❶ Following directions on page 132, prepare a background square with light creases for centering the appliqué. Mark the position of the centers of the stems; use dots to indicate the points of the petals.

❷ Using the tulip template on page 176, cut and prepare flower and leaf pieces by finger-creasing. For the stems, cut one strip on the straight grain, 4½ inches long x ¾ inch wide. Cut two strips on the bias, 2½ x ¾ inch. Press under a ¼-inch seam allowance.

❸ Position the curved stems, then blind-hem down both sides with matching color thread. The raw ends that will be covered by subsequent pieces do not have to be turned under. Position the straight stem so that it covers the ends of the curved stems, trimming if necessary, then baste.

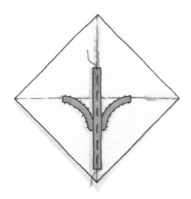

❹ Pin on the first leaf, right side up, tucking one end under the basted stem. Starting on one longer side, stroke the seam allowance under with the tip of your needle as far as the pencil line and hold securely in place with your thumb.

Bring the needle up from the back of the block into the edge of the leaf and proceed to blind-hem (see page 135). Work around the whole shape, stroking under each small section before sewing. Avoid pulling the stitches too tight, as this will crimp or pucker the fabric.

❺ Work the second leaf in the same way, then blind-hem the center stem, turning under about ⅛ inch to neaten the lower end.

**6** Pin petal A to the background block and turn under the top edge only. For the point, blind-hem along one side of the pencil line right to the point. With the tip of your needle, fold under the unsewn seam allowance. Continue sewing the other side. Baste the sections that will be covered by petals B and Br.

**Above:** Detail of *Princess Feather*, American, early nineteenth century.

**7** Position and pin petal B following the same instructions for sewing points as described in step 6. Be sure it covers the raw edge of the center stem. For smooth results when sewing the concave shapes, clip into the seam allowance just before sewing.

### TIP

● To make quilting easier, trim away the background from behind appliquéd shapes. Do this very carefully, separating the two layers with a pin to avoid cutting into the motif when entering from the background fabric.

Trim, leaving a scant ¼-inch seam allowance of background within the stitched outline. If you plan to do this, it is best done as you work. Otherwise, if you have several shapes overlapping, it will be difficult to cut away neatly and will leave you with various thicknesses behind the design.

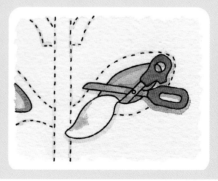

**8** Finish the appliqué block by adding petal Br in the same manner. Work the two other tulip blooms in the same way.

# RAW-EDGED APPLIQUÉ

As the name suggests, raw-edged appliqué shapes are applied without having the raw edges turned under. Shapes are cut out with pinking shears, pinking blade, or wave blade of a rotary cutter. This easy method suits the skills of a beginner and is an ideal introduction to appliqué.

**Above:** Detail of *Skittish Robin*, by Jenni Dobson, English, twentieth century. Techniques used to make this quilt are explained below.

## Making a Sample Block

① From the patterns provided on page 176, make templates for the leaves and the robin.

② Place each template right side up on an appropriately colored scrap and draw an outline. Cut out the leaves, whole body, and red robin breast with pinking shears or the decorative blade of a rotary cutter; do not add seam allowances. To each wing add a ¼-inch turning on one side to tuck under the body.

③ Cut one 6-inch square for the background.

④ Arrange the body and wings on the background, with the wings just tucked under the body on each side. Pin or baste. Sew with hand or machine running stitches ⅛ inch along the inside of the edge of each shape. Sew the wings, then the body, the breast, and the holly leaves.

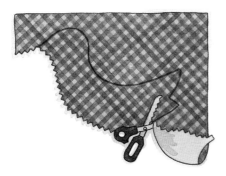

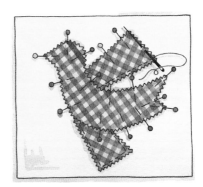

⑤ Embroider the bird's legs with stem stitch and the eye with a French knot.

**Above:** *Baltimore Basket,* Rosalind Sutton, English, twentieth
century. For instructions on how to make this quilt, see page 142.

# FREEZER PAPER APPLIQUÉ

Freezer paper is a moisture- and vapor-proof product used for wrapping food for freezing. Quilt-makers use freezer paper to act as a template, which is ironed, waxy side facing the fabric, and removed from the work before the final stitches are made. Using freezer paper eliminates the need to mark your fabric and gives a defined edge with which to turn under the fabric before sewing it down. It is not practical to use freezer paper for making stems; their narrowness would make the template very difficult to remove.

## Making a Sample Rose and Leaf Cluster Block

**1** Prepare an 8-inch background square of muslin. Lightly mark the points and junctions of leaves and petals with a pencil dot.

**2** From the template, trace the appliqué shapes in reverse onto the paper side of the freezer paper. Cut out the shapes on the drawn line without seam allowances.

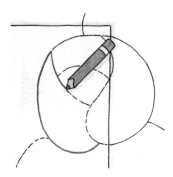

**3** Iron each shape with the waxy side facing the wrong side of the fabric, spacing shapes to allow a ¼-inch seam allowance all around. Cut out, adding the turning by eye.

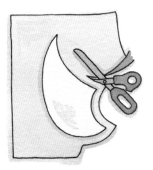

**4** Position the leaves first, following the sequence marked on the template. Hold the shape in place with a pin, a tiny dab of glue stick or a couple of basting stitches. Fold the seam allowance to the wrong side and blind-hem the motif to the background.

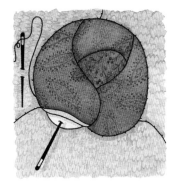

**5** Remove the freezer paper just before securing the last stitches.

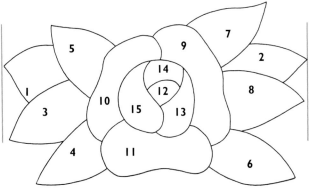

Template of Rose and Leaf Cluster. Enlarge to measure 7 inches between the two blue lines.

# baltimore basket
**made by Rosalind Sutton**

## MATERIALS
- 4½ yd. backing
- 85 x 85 in. (minimum) batting
- 4 yd. muslin
- 2 yd. burgundy print
- ½ yd. deep rose for the basket lining
- ⅜ yd. burgundy/rose texture print for the basket strips
- Fat quarters for the leaves and flowers—medium and dark green prints x 9; light and medium blue prints x 8; deep rose or red prints x 4; light pinks x 5; yellow/gold/ocher prints x 4; beige on cream prints x 2; peach with green x 1; black on blue x 1
- Scraps of one turquoise print and one solid turquoise for bows
- Sewing and quilting thread
- Freezer paper

**Finished size** 73 x 73 in.

## CUTTING
- From the patterns provided on pages 178–184, make freezer paper templates for all motifs, tracing each in reverse. Iron to the fabric, then cut out the shapes. Freezer-paper templates can be used more than once. Cut more as required. Templates are not needed for the basket strips. From template plastic, cut templates for the basket base, body, and top edge.

## MUSLIN
- Cut two outer borders, each 76 x 16 in. These are oversized on both length and width to allow for take-up.
- Cut two borders, each 46 x 16 in.—these are equally oversized in width as the side borders but are only ½ in. longer.
- Cut two inner borders 44 x 8½ in. and two 28 x 8½ in.
- Cut the center medallion 28 x 28 in.

## BURGUNDY
- Cut eight strips, 1½ in. wide, across the full width of the fabric and set aside for binding to finish ⅜ in. wide.

- Cut five strips, 1½ in. wide, across the full width of the fabric for framing.
- Using the freezer-paper templates, cut the ribbon border: four corner knots, two tails, 14 straight knots, and 16 ribbon swags. Cut center stretch swag later to fit space available exactly.
- Using templates, cut one basket base, one basket top edge, and one strip 1⅛ x 15 in., to be pressed into thirds along its length for weaving into the basket.

- Cut some of the flowers or petals in the basket or garlands from leftover scraps.

## BASKET FABRICS
- Using the template on page 184, cut one basket from deep rose solid.
- From the rose and burgundy print, cut 26 straight-grain strips, each 1⅛-in. wide by 11 in. long. Press into thirds lengthwise.

## TURQUOISE PRINT AND SOLID
- With templates, cut four sets of print and solid pieces for the bows.

## FAT QUARTERS FOR FLOWERS, LEAVES, AND STEMS
- The garland appears five times in the quilt. To make them identical, cut five of each petal, flower, and leaf. Label and store each piece until needed.
- Using your freezer-paper templates, cut leaves, flowers, and petals to fill the basket. You can cut all before sewing or cut a few at a time.
- To make very narrow stems, as required for the spray on the left, cut strips 1 in. wide and press in half.

## Sewing

1 Lightly mark the 28-in. square for the center medallion, following the instructions in Preparation for Hand Appliqué on page 132. Baste the basket to the background. Position and baste the vertical basket strips, beginning in the center. Weave the horizontal strip through the vertical strips, then blind-hem all the strips in place. Leave the sides of the horizontal strip unstitched for a more three-dimensional appearance. Add the base and top edge of the basket.

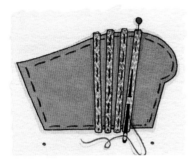

2 Fill the basket with leaves and flowers. Study the design carefully and work out your sewing sequence. Apply the underneath shapes first, then those that will be overlapped by other shapes. Remember that any parts that are overlapped should not be turned under. Remove the freezer-paper templates as you complete each shape.

3 For the narrow stems, position the strip pressed in half earlier over the stitching line so that it will be closer to the fold at the top and so that the folded fabric represents the desired finished width of stem. Sew along the stitching line using a running backstitch. Trim the excess raw edge so that it fits under the fold when the stem is flipped over. Blind-hem to the background.

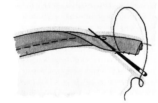

4 Trim the medallion to 27½ in. square. Attach the inner-border strips with ¼-in. seam allowances. Press the seams open. Over these work the four corner garlands. Add the turquoise bows. The medallion with borders measures 43½ x 43½ in.

5 Attach the burgundy framing strips, joining as necessary to achieve the required length. The framed medallion should measure 45½ x 45½ in.

6 Work the fifth garland centered on the top outer-border strip.

7 Work as much as possible of the ribbon appliqué along the two long side borders. (A corner knot at both ends and five knots connected by six swags of ribbon.)

8 Center the top appliqué border on the top edge of the medallion and attach. Add the empty outer border to the bottom. Match the midpoint of the long side borders to the midpoint of the medallion and check that the ribbons balance on opposite sides of the quilt before sewing.

9 To complete the lower ribbon border, prepare, pin, and baste into place the remaining four knots and swags, placing them to connect with the corner knots. Measure the center space and cut a stretched swag accordingly. Stitch this assembled lower border, then add the single rose motif.

10 Complete the ribbon border by adding the tails over the seams at the top of the quilt.

11 For the quilting mark a ⅜-in. grid in the medallion, and for the border parallel lines ½ in. apart.

## Finishing

1 Divide the backing fabric into two pieces and join. Assemble the quilt layers and baste. Protect the outer edges by folding the excess backing over to enclose the batting. Then quilt, working from the center outward.

2 The finished quilt should measure 73 x 73 in., with outer borders of 14¼ in. Insert a line of basting within the seam allowance.

3 The 1½-in.-wide binding should be attached with raw edges level with the quilt edge. Sew with a ⅜-in. seam. Fold over to the back, turn in ⅜ in., and blind-hem to finish ⅜ in. wide.

4 Make a hanging sleeve. Sign and date your quilt.

**Above:** Broderie Perse bedspread, English, early nineteenth century.

# BRODERIE PERSE

Named because of its similarities to Persian embroidery, this technique was immensely popular during the eighteenth and early nineteenth century, probably originating with the arrival of colorfast chintzes imported from India. These exotic fabrics enchanted the European public, who were accustomed to inferior cottons. Chintzes were expensive, and when imports were banned, they became harder to come by. Hence, no scraps were too small to be used. Arrange motifs cut from printed fabrics into new designs on a plain background using blind-hem stitch with a narrow turning, or decorative buttonhole, stitch.

## Making a Sample with Buttonhole Stitch

❶ Collect a selection of printed fabrics. Home-furnishing fabrics offer a good variety of strong color and motifs. Avoid thick fabrics, fabrics with a loose weave, linen blends, and satin weaves. Cottons similar to dressweight fabrics are best. You'll also need a square of background fabric and some embroidery thread. Choose colors closest to those of the printed motif.

**Above:** Detail of Broderie Perse, by Jo Davey, English, twentieth century.

❷ Wash and press your fabrics.

❸ Working with very sharp scissors, accurately cut out your motifs. A cleanly cut edge is important. Go for bold designs for maximum effect, leaving small and intricate shapes until you are confident that you can handle them with ease. Small details, such as stems or tendrils, can always be embroidered later.

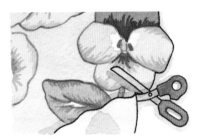

❹ Arrange the motifs into a new design on the background fabric. Baste in place.

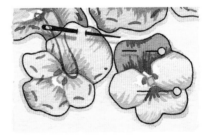

❺ Work a close buttonhole stitch around the outside of the shapes (see page 135). When sewing around curves, use a wider stitch.

❻ Remove the basting stitches. Place the work face down and press lightly (see page 36).

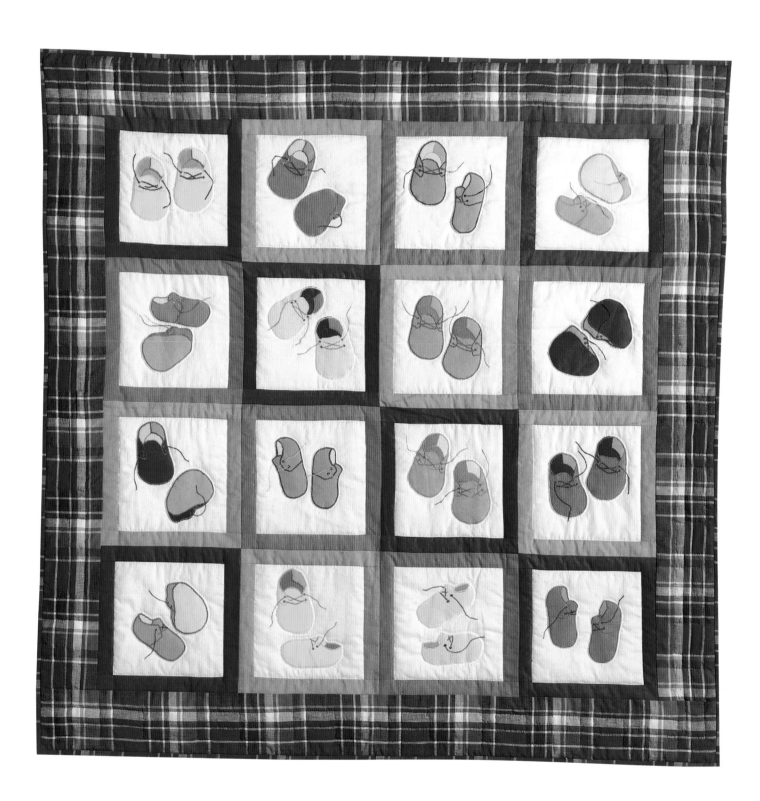

**Above:** *First Steps Baby Quilt*, by Patricia Payn, English, late twentieth century. The technique used in making this quilt is explained opposite.

# FUSIBLE WEB APPLIQUÉ

Machine appliqué is much simpler these days owing to the development of fusible-web products. When fused to fabric by the application of heat, fusible web provides stability to the appliqué motif and seals the edges against fraying.

## Machine Appliqué Sample Using Fusible Web

When fused to the wrong side of the appliqué and then to the background fabric, manufacturers claim items are secure without any further stitching. However, it is recommended that the edges of any item subject to wear, handling, and washing be machine sewn with a zigzag or satin stitch. Be sure to have the web side facing the fabric and the paper side up toward the iron or you will have a sticky mess to clean up! Protect the layers with a piece of baking parchment. Beginners to the technique should use a paper-supported fusible web. Follow the individual manufacturer's instructions. When working with delicate or heat-sensitive fabrics, protect them from the direct heat of the iron by using either paper or a pressing cloth.

❶ Cut a square of cotton fabric for the background and collect a variety of cotton scraps for the appliqué. If necessary, enlarge your motif to at least 4 inches, or larger if preferred.

❷ Because the web will be fixed to the wrong side of the appliqué motifs, the pattern must be traced in reverse. Turn the pattern over and ink in the lines on the back of the paper. Label this side "working side." Place the fusible web with its paper side up over the working side of the design and in pencil trace around each part of the design separately.

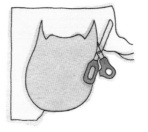

❸ Cut out each piece without seam allowances.

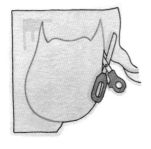

❹ With an iron set on cotton, fuse each webbing shape to the wrong side of the fabric with the paper side up. Allow the pieces to become thoroughly cool before handling.

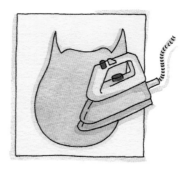

❺ Cut out each of the pieces without seam allowances.

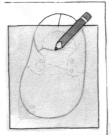

❻ With the background block right side up, position all the pieces, peeling away the paper backing and placing them right side up. There should be no gaps between the component parts. When all the shapes are in place, carefully bond the motifs to the background block, following the manufacturer's instructions.

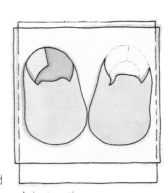

❼ Work machine zigzag or satin stitch around the shapes, choosing matching thread or some of the shaded or variegated threads available. Work a stitch test, as the tension may need to be set slightly looser than for regular sewing. Avoid setting the stitch length too close together, as the stitching may bunch up. When sewing curves, guide the fabric so that the machine sews without stopping; this prevents layers of stitches from piling up.

**Above:** *Hawaiian Small Quilt*, by Maggie Davies, English,
late twentieth century. The technique used to make this quilt
is explained opposite.

# HAWAIIAN APPLIQUÉ

The Hawaiian quilt is characterized by its design, generally an eight-fold repeat reminiscent of the paper cutouts many of us made as children. In the same way, Hawaiian quilters cut into the whole piece of folded cloth. This large single design is worked in one solid color and appliquéd with a blind-hem stitch to a white background. The designs are often intricate and take their inspiration from local flora. Figurative images are considered unlucky. Tradition has it that each quilt top (*kapa lau*) must be a unique design—copying another's pattern is frowned upon by the Hawaiian quilting community.

## Making a 12-inch Block

**1** Fold a 12-inch square of paper three times (fig. 1). Draw a design with connecting parts on the folded edges. Shade in the parts to be cut out. Staple the parts to be cut away to prevent the paper from shifting while cutting (fig. 2).

**5** Cut out the shape, adding a ¼-inch turning. The cut fabric should be handled as little as possible to avoid stretching its shaped edges.

**fig. 1**                    **fig. 2**

**2** Cut out your design and unfold. Refold the design three times as before. The design can be revised by refolding the paper and making further cuts.

**3** Make a template of the folded design (one-eighth of the whole).

**4** Fold a 12-inch square of a single color fabric in the same way that you folded the paper. Press between each fold, then baste layers in place. Position the template, draw around it, and baste again within the design area.

**6** Unfold and center, right side up, over the right side of the 13-inch background square. Pin and baste the appliqué ⅜ inch away from the edges.

**7** Begin sewing the marked section, working from the center outward. Clip into the seam allowance on concave curves as you come to them. Needle-turn the edge under along the drawn line, then blind-hem with thread that matches the top fabric.

**8** Layer the block, then echo-quilt around the appliqué (see page 158).

# MOLA APPLIQUÉ

A close relative of reverse appliqué, this method also involves working with several layers of fabric, building up the design from the bottom and cutting away parts of the top layer. The style is associated with the San Blas islands off the coast of Panama; a mola is a woman's blouse that has been decorated with a reverse appliqué panel. The main effect is of shapes echoed by successive outlines of color. Mola work includes inlay, a technique in which small slits are made in the top layer of fabric and contrasting colors are inserted.

## Making a Sample Block

**1** Assemble solid black, blue, ocher, and red 100 percent cotton fabric scraps, each approximately 11 x 7 inches; tracing paper; and sewing and embroidery thread. Always match thread to the fabric being applied.

**2** Cut an 11 x 7-inch rectangle of black fabric for the background.

**3** Place a layer of blue fabric right side up over the right side of the black. Pin or baste the layers together. Make a tracing of the large cat-body pattern (see page 177). Baste the tracing over the blue and, with basting thread, work running stitches along the design lines as a guide to blind-hemming.

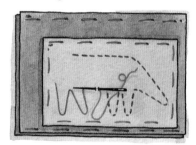

**4** Carefully tear away the tracing, leaving the design marked in thread underneath.

**5** Cut into the top layer (blue) about ⅛ inch away from the running-stitch line outside the cat shape.

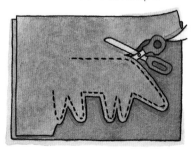

**6** Needle-turn under and blind-hem, cutting the marker running stitches as you go. Keep your stitching close together. Clip into tight corners as necessary. Remove excess fabric.

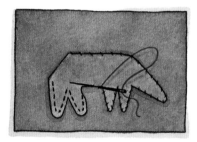

**7** To add a third color (ocher) outside the cat, cut a rectangle at least 1 inch larger than the hemmed shape. Baste in position, right side up.

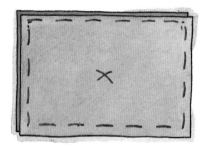

**8** The stitched cat outline will appear on the back of the work. Working ⅛ inch outside this outline, baste a line of running stitches through all layers; this marks where the new color will be hemmed.

⑨ Turn back to the top of the work and cut ⅛ inch inside the line. Turn in the edge and blind-hem to the line, removing the stitches as you go. This leaves a black channel ⅛ inch wide between the two colors.

⑩ Place the fourth (red) rectangle over the panel, right side up. Pin or baste the layers (fig. 1).

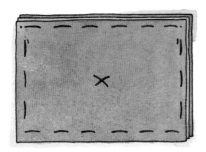

**fig. 1**

Turn the work to the back. The cat should be visible as parallel lines of stitching in two different colors—blue inner line and ocher outer line. With basting thread and a running stitch, mark around the cat, inside and outside, ⅛ inch away from the respective lines of stitching (fig. 2).

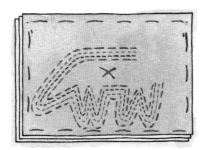

**fig. 2**

Be sure to go through all layers so that it is visible on the top (red) when you turn the panel right side up.

The running-stitch lines mark where you will blind-hem. Cut ⅛ inch away from the lines, inside or outside as appropriate, turn under, and blind-hem the raw edge (fig. 3).

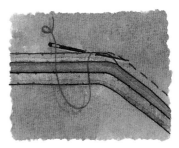

**fig. 3**

⑪ Using the conventional needle turning method, appliqué the cat's head, first in blue, then in red, over the raw edges of the neck.

⑫ Decorate the area around the cat with triangles of inlay (see detail below). Into the red make a small three-way cut and insert a scrap of another color. Turn under the little points of the top layer and blind-hem.

⑬ Embroider such details as whiskers and eyes with a running stitch.

⑭ Back and bind the block to finish.

# mola wall hanging

**made by Anne Tuck**

## MATERIALS
- 1½ yd. black for backing
- 1 yd. garnet red
- ¾ yd. blue
- ¾ yd. ocher
- ½ yd. pink
- ¼ yd. ocher and rust stripe
- ¼ yd. emerald green
- ¼ yd. warm yellow
- ⅛ yd. dark green
- Basting, sewing, and embroidery thread

**Finished size 32 x 26 in.**

## CUTTING
### BLACK
- Cut a piece 33 x 27 in. for backing.
- Cut a rectangle 30 x 24 in. for the background.

- Cut two strips ⅞ x 30 in. and two strips ⅞ x 24 in. for the inner borders.
- From the templates provided on pages 176–177, enlarge the design for the cats' heads, bodies, and leaf twigs.

### GARNET RED
- Cut a rectangle 30 x 24 in.
- Cut two strips 1¾ x 33 in. and two strips 1¾ x 25 in. for the outer border.
- Cut strips 1¼ in. wide to total 120 in. for the binding.

### BLUE
- Cut a rectangle 30 x 24 in.
- The remaining pieces are cut later.

## Sewing

**1** On the black background mark the design areas with basting; use the photograph as a guide.

**2** For the center panel, make tracings of the cat body: two facing left and one facing right. For the borders, make four tracings of the front-view body and four of the back-view body.

**3** Place the second layer of fabric (blue) right side up over the right side of the black. Baste the layers together, including a line around the central area of the panel. One at a time, baste the tracings in place over the blue and, with basting thread, work running stitches along the design lines. Mark the center side-view cats, the lower back-view cat in the left-hand border, and the top back-view cat in the right-hand border. Tear away the tracings.

**4** Cut into the blue ⅛ in. away from the running-stitch line outside the first center cat shape. Needle-turn under and blind-hem. Repeat for the two other center cats.

**5** Repeat the process to cut and turn in the blue around the central area toward the border side. There will be some blue fabric in the center that can now be removed.

**6** Repeat the process for the lower-left and top-right side cats.

**7** The remaining border cats have yellow or pink bodies, so they need a slightly different treatment. Begin with the top left-hand side cat. Remove the blue rectangle from the appropriate basted area. Keep intact, as it will be used in step 11 to help vary the cats' color scheme. Into the space, put an equivalent piece of warm yellow. Baste a front cat-body tracing on top. With running stitches and basting thread, mark the outline. Cut ⅛ in. away outside the running stitches, then blind-hem into place, again removing the running stitches as you go. In the same way, work the lower right-hand side cat.

**8** Repeat step 7 to work the pink cats on the top and bottom borders. All the cats should now have body shapes against the black background.

**9** Baste and appliqué strips of striped fabric on the inner side of the center panel and on the small side panels. These will have some raw edges, which will be covered by the red layer.

**10** To add the ocher outside the center cat, cut a rectangle at least 1 in. larger than the hemmed shape. Pin or baste in position right side up and proceed as in step 4 on page 150. Repeat to add pink around the top and bottom center cats.

**11** To add blue outside the first yellow cat, replace the rectangle removed earlier. Repeat step 10 to add blue outside the pink cats on the bottom left and top right. Add ocher outside the remaining top, bottom, and side cats.

**12** Place the red rectangle over the panel, right side up. Baste the layers and proceed as in step 5 on page 150. To complete the fourth layer, repeat marking and sewing around the separate panels.

**13** Over the raw edges of the necks on the center cats, appliqué the heads, first in blue, then red.

**14** Cut and apply the leafy twigs. Add separate leaves and chain stitch the stems.

**15** Decorate the background with pebble shapes and inlay triangles in bright colors (see step 12 on page 151). To make a pebble, mark an oval and baste the center. Cut along the marked line. Needle-turn the red fabric away from the line on both sides and blind-hem to secure.

**16** Using the photograph opposite as a guide, embroider the details and add the beads.

## Finishing

**1** Trim the panel to 23½ x 29¼ in. Attach the narrow black inner-border strips to all four sides. Add the red outer borders (see page 42).

**2** Place the backing right side down with the panel on top right side up. Baste all around the edges. Add the binding, turn it over to the back and blind-hem in place.

**3** Make and attach a hanging sleeve (see page 57). Sign and date the wall hanging.

# STAINED GLASS APPLIQUÉ

To create the appearance of stained glass in fabrics, narrow strips of black bias representing the lead are appliquéd around the colored fabric shapes. Although black is the most common choice for the bias strips between the shapes, it is possible to choose other dark shades. The bias strips are usually applied by hand, although they can be blind-hemmed by machine.

## Making a Sample Turtledove Block

❶ Assemble a square of light-colored background fabric and scraps of colors for the glass. You also need a 15-inch square of a fine black cotton fabric for the lead, along with basting and black sewing thread.

❷ Enlarge the design on page 174 to a diameter of 10 inches. Decide on the color placement and label the appliqué shapes accordingly.

❸ Take each color in turn and, matching the grain line of the appliqué to that of the background, place right side up over the design and trace off the relevant shape (fig. 1).

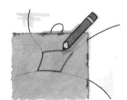

**fig. 1**

Where adjacent shapes are the same color, cut as one piece but mark the lines between the parts (fig. 2).

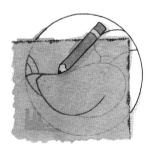

**fig. 2**

Also trace details like veins on leaves when they exist in the design. Leave space between each piece for cutting with a scant ⅛-inch seam allowance (fig. 3). For dark fabrics, trace and cut out a paper template first to use for marking. To mark detail lines, cut the template and trace along the required edge.

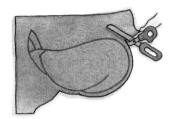

**fig. 3**

❹ Tape the background fabric, right side up, over the design and trace with a fine pencil line.

❺ Pin each appliqué piece over the design (fig. 4). The pencil outlines on the shapes should exactly match with those on the background. Where two fabrics meet, their seam allowances will overlap and all the pencil lines should coincide.

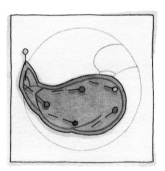

**fig. 4**

❻ With running stitches, baste all the edges along the pencil lines through all the layers (fig. 5). These stitches remain in the work and will be covered by the bias later.

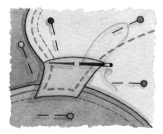

**fig. 5**

**7** Do not use purchased bias tape for stained-glass appliqué. Prepare bias in the following manner:

**(a)** Using the 45° angle on your quilter's ruler or a set square, cut a triangle shape from the corner of the black fabric. Lay the ruler overlapping the bias edge by ¾ inch and cut off a strip. Repeat to cut several strips. Cut more strips as needed to complete the design.

**(b)** Prepare strips by placing right side down as directed on pages 135 and 137. If your first attempt is wobbly, spray with a fine mist of water and try again. Avoid distorting the strip.

**8** Work one strip at a time. Plan ahead to determine the sequence of strips to ensure neat ends and unnecessary overlapping of strips.

**9** With the raw edge down, pin, then blind-hem around the appliqué shape (fig. 6).

**fig. 6**

Where possible, sew inside curves first. If there is a sharp angle, fold the bias like a miter, although the angle must suit the design. Add an extra stitch across this fold to secure it as invisibly as you can. Sometimes a strip may be partly sewn with a gap left along one side to accommodate another strip that will be tucked in later (fig. 7).

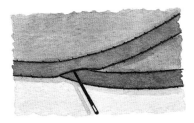

**fig. 7**

**10** If an end will be covered by another strip, trim to ⅛ inch then continue with the next strip in sequence until the design is complete.

**11** If your machine has a blind-hem stitch, it can be used to attach the bias strips. Work as for the hand method; remember, though, that the bias strips need to be basted in place before machine blind-hemming. Always work a test s

**Above:** Detail of stained glass window hanging, by Jo Davey, English, twentieth century.

first to make sure the tension is not too tight and that the stitch will penetrate the bias without being conspicuous. A satin stitch or appliqué foot may feed the work through the machine more evenly.

**12** Make a French knot for the eye with stranded embroidery thread.

# QUILTING TECHNIQUES

The continuous running stitch that holds the layers of fabric and filling together is known as quilting. Depending on the design of the quilt and the quilter's skill, the quilting plan can be plain and unobtrusive, simply following the seams of the piecing, or it can be very elaborate, filled with intricate patterns of wreaths, feathers, and flowers. Simple pieced designs of solid-color fabrics or whole cloth quilts encourage intricate showcase quilting. These very elaborate quilting designs are favored by the Amish, Welsh, and northern English communities—each producing designs of outstanding beauty.

Much of the romance associated with quilt-making comes from our knowledge of the quilting bee. This gathering of friends, family, and neighbors functioned on two levels: first, as an expedient way of quilting tops that had been pieced during winter months—the dextrous fingers of five or six women around a frame could finish a quilt very quickly—and second, as a social occasion that offered a break from the chores of everyday life.

**Left:** Detail of *Cockscomb and Currant* variation, American, ca.1850.

# PREPARATION FOR QUILTING

Whether you intend to hand or machine quilt or use a combination of both, good preparation is vital. Decisions must be made about the quilting design and how it will be marked. The quilt layers must be assembled and secured.

## Batting

In the past, quilt fillings have included lambswool, blankets, worn quilts, or whatever was on hand. Recent years have seen a tremendous increase in the variety of batting available. Batting is described by its fiber content and weight. All commercially available batting must conform to minimum flame retardancy regulations. This means that it will not burn faster than a predetermined rate. The most widely used fiber for batting is polyester. Its stability means the quilting lines can be stitched farther apart without fear of the batting shifting. Polyester also extends the life of a quilt. Cotton, wool, or silk battings often contain a percentage of the fiber for this reason. Some battings with a high proportion of cotton will shrink when washed. Prewash these varieties before sewing. If you intend to give your quilt an "antique" appearance, use a cotton batting but do not prewash it. The batting will shrink causing the quilt top to wrinkle.

Whether you plan to hand or machine quilt will affect the choice of batting used. Batting is often described in terms of its weight, such as 2- or 4-ounce, but it can be compressed in the manufacturing process so that the same weight appears thinner. This is known as "low-loft" batting and is very good for machine quilting. Thick and fluffy batting is called "high-loft" and is a popular filling for comforters, children's quilts, or tied projects. For wall hangings and clothing, use needlepunched batting. It is very stable and hangs well.

Batting is sold off the roll in various widths and also in precut pieces suitable for all bed-size quilts. Natural-fiber batting comes in white or off-white, but a charcoal-colored version is available for use with quilt tops of mainly dark colors. Occasionally, tiny fibers from the batting work their way through to the top and create a hazy coating over the surface. This process is called "bearding" and is more noticeable on dark fabrics. If bearding happens, lightly "shave" the surface with a razor—do not pull the fibers out. Store batting with as few folds as possible. A day or two before you plan to use it, spread it out to encourage any creases to fall out.

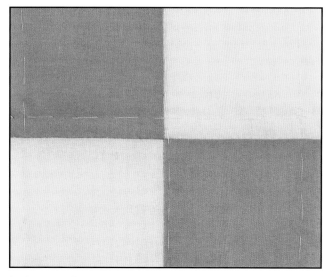

In-the-ditch Quilting

## Choosing the Design

Quilting may simply follow the design of a pieced or appliqué top—outline, in-the-ditch, and echo-quilting. All three are popular because none need additional marking. In-the-ditch refers to sewing along the seam lines or, in the case of appliqué, right next to the applied shapes. It is particularly good for beginners, as the actual stitches cannot be seen—only their effect.

Outline quilting is stitched ¼ inch away from the seam, appliqué design, or printed motif on the fabric. Echo-quilting is an echoing series of quilting lines stitched around the patchwork or appliqué shapes. Echo-quilting is stitched ¼ inch away from the shape with all further quilting lines equally spaced. The effect is to throw the enclosed design into higher relief. It is an easy method for beginners who are ready to show off their improving stitches.

Outline Quilting

Other quilting patterns fall into three main groups: motifs, such as wreaths and flowers, often used centered in blocks or panels; running patterns, such as cables and running feathers, which contribute movement to a design and are often used in borders; and filling patterns.

Fillings are simple patterns often based on grids and used to fill in background areas. They provide an overall texture without distracting from the main design.

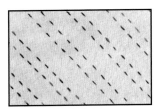 

Filling Quilting Patterns

## Using Quilting Templates and Stencils

A template is a shape that is a guide for drawing; it suits simple motifs. If a shape is to be traced around many times, it should be made of durable material, such as template plastic.

Templates can include very simple forms that tessellate to make overall patterns and grids or that build into running patterns, such as a teardrop used to draft feather designs.

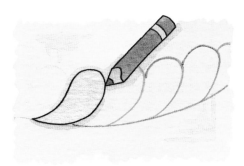

To mark the quilting pattern, place the template on a paper draft of the quilt, if at the designing stage, or directly on the quilt top, and draw around it. Move to the next position and repeat. With tessellating designs, place the template against one of the lines already marked and draw around the remaining shape. Such designs often need one or more baselines—these should not be drawn; instead, finger-press a line or add a strip of masking tape.

A stencil is a sheet of plastic with channels cut into it, along which you run your marking tool. It suits running designs like cables. On commercial stencils, the channels are interrupted by bars that help keep the design whole. They are also marked with center lines and balance marks.

When using templates or stencils, keep track of which way the design is going. When a design turns a corner, it often becomes a mirror image of itself. This indicates that the template or stencil needs to be flipped over.

## Marking

First test the design against the intended space, marking repeats with pins. This avoids making a large adjustment to one single repeat. Decide how best to fit the design. It can be stretched or compressed. It may be better to have one less repeat and to stretch the last two or three repeats, or else have an extra repeat and compress them.

Mark your quilt as little as possible, using the simplest marking methods, such as an H grade graphite pencil on light or medium fabrics. For dark fabrics, try a sliver of dry soap or a light or silver pencil. Whichever marker you use, keep it well sharpened to maintain a fine, accurate line. For marking filling patterns, masking tape is useful and avoids having to draw many lines on your quilt. Only tape what you can sew in one sitting. Never leave tape on the quilt for any length of time or in bright sunlight. Simply place a length of tape on the proposed quilting line and quilt alongside.

Self-adhesive plastic is suitable for making templates to your own specifications. Such templates can be used and repositioned several times before they no longer adhere. The same warning as for masking tape applies here. An alternative is to draw the design on tracing paper and baste it to the quilt. Quilt the design through the paper, by hand or by machine, then tear the paper away. This allows you to add a design on an already layered quilt top.

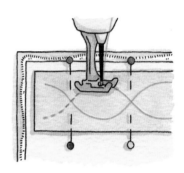

## Fudging

This term refers to modifying a design in subtle ways to make it fit an available space. In an ideal world, the quilting design is drafted to fit the project; however, you may be working with purchased templates whose size does not fit exactly into the space.

Because fudging means redrawing parts of the design, it is best to use the template for drawing the most complex parts. This helps fool the eye into thinking things are perfect! Then, to make the necessary changes, draw the simplest parts freehand to fit the space. Draw part of the template, then slip it to one side to continue drawing and to connect the parts freehand.

## Using Hoops and Frames

After the quilt has been marked and layered, it is ready for quilting. Some experienced quilters are happy to quilt without the assistance of a frame. However, beginners will find a frame or hoop invaluable. A hoop stabilizes the quilt layers, helping to create even tension and achieve a more consistent surface appearance.

A hoop consists of two wooden round or oval rings with a screw adjuster on the outer ring. Bind wooden hoops with cotton tape to avoid wood stains and to give good grip on the fabric. The hoop is moved from place to place over the quilt and keeps the work easily portable. Avoid overtightening; this can distort the quilt. Never leave the quilt fixed in the hoop when not quilting, as doing so can mark or distort the fabrics.

A freestanding wooden frame in which the quilt layers are fixed for the entire quilting process provides the most even surface and allows several quilters to work at the same time.

Smaller embroidery hoops or rings are useful for free-motion machine quilting. Some sewing machines will not form good stitches unless the layers are tensioned in an embroidery ring. The ring is moved from one part to another as work progresses.

**Above:** *Diamond in a Square*, American Amish, nineteenth century.

# MACHINE QUILTING

Machine quilting necessitates preparation different from that of hand quilting, but it requires the same amount of practice to do well. Although it is possible to quilt with an all-purpose presser foot, a walking or an even-feed foot encourages the three layers of the sandwich to pass through the machine at the same rate.

**1** Use a size 80 needle and a regular mercerized-cotton sewing thread. Make a sandwich of muslin and batting to test your machine settings. Low-loft cotton batting is recommended because cotton fabrics cling to it, reducing the amount of basting required and limiting the amount of movement that takes place.

**2** Use safety pins for basting the layers. They can be removed or repositioned quickly during stitching. If thread-basting, put the basting to one side of where you plan to quilt. Basting threads pierced by the quilting stitches are difficult to remove.

**3** Sew a short line on the sample to check stitch length—usually 8–10 stitches per inch. Fabric can tear away from stitches that are too small, and large stitches do not have enough stretch to tolerate stress on the quilt during use.

**4** When the stitch length is right, examine the tension. Because the quilt sandwich is thicker than a normal two-fabric layer, you may need to reduce the tension a little; however, the two threads should still lock together in the middle. This may be easier to see if you load different colors on top and in the bobbin for testing.

## Free-motion Quilting

- Study your sewing-machine manual for free-motion stitching advice.
- Fit a darning or free-embroidery foot if available, or remove foot—and keep your fingers well away from the needle!
- Drop feed dogs or cover with special throat plate.
- Some machines require work to be fashioned in an embroidery hoop to form good free-motion stitching.

**5** Check whether your machine has a control to alter the amount of downward pressure on the presser foot. Machines are set for sewing two layers of fabric. As the quilt sandwich is thicker, it fills the space under the presser foot more, and slightly less pressure is needed. This reduces the tendency of the machine to push the layers through at different rates, which can cause the quilt to pucker.

**6** Continuous lines make the quilting go more quickly and eliminate having to finish many thread ends. Practice tracing over designs to see how they can be modified for continuous stitching.

**7** When beginning to sew, turn the balance wheel to insert the needle at the right place and draw the bobbin thread to the top. Hold both threads as you begin to sew to avoid the lower one becoming tangled underneath.

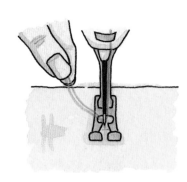

**8** As you guide the work through the machine, hold it on each side of the needle with your fingertips and exert slight sideways pressure. On pieced tops, this opens up the ditch a little, helping the stitches to sink into the seam. Such tension also helps with free-motion work, reducing the need to fit the work into an embroidery hoop.

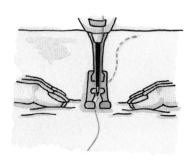

**9** To reduce the effort of trimming the threads at the beginning and end of a line of stitching, set the machine stitch length to almost 0. Run the machine for a stitch or two, then increase the length to normal, preferably while slowly running the machine. Sew the line to about ¾–1 inch from the end, then reduce the stitch length again to almost 0. Cut the threads, leaving tails of 2½–3 inches. Thread both tails through a needle with a large eye. Insert the needle into the batting only at the stitching and bring it out again a short distance away (fig. 1). Tension these slightly as you snip them so that they will pop back inside and be hidden (fig. 2).

**fig. 1**                    **fig. 2**

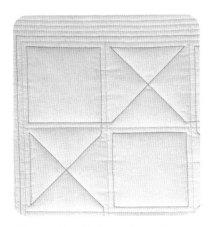

**Above:** Detail of machine quilting.

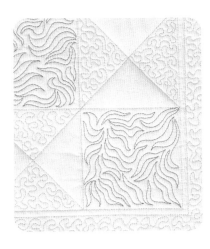

**Above:** Detail of free-motion machine quilting. Both details by C. June Barnes.

**Above:** Detail of *Folk Art Meets Jazz*, with echo quilting, by Katharine Guerrier, English, twentieth century.

# diamond in a square

made by
**Angela Guppy**

## Quilt-as-you-go

A more accurate term would be "quilt-as-you-piece." However, the term is widely accepted for a technique where the backing and batting are basted together, then the piecing, placed on top is sewn through all the layers. The method gives a quilted effect at the same time as assembling the design. Pieced sections can be joined together, as with the frames below, before adding to the quilt and extra quilting may be added later to create symmetry of quilting patterns.

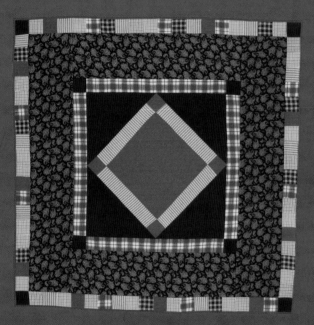

### MATERIALS
- 1⅞ yd. 70-in.-wide muslin (minimum)
- 85 × 85 in. (minimum) lightweight batting
- ¾ yd. red cotton flannel (includes binding)
- ¾ yd. dark teal blue cotton flannel
- 1¾ yd. cotton flannel print for wide border
- ½ yd. each five different cotton flannel plaids or stripes
- Thread for sewing

**Finished size**  approximately 60 × 60 in.

### PREPARATION
- Iron the backing, which should be 4–6 in. larger than the desired finished size. Place right side down on a flat surface.
- Center a same size batting on top. Pin and baste without knotting the thread ends. In a different color thread, mark accurate center lines vertically and horizontally. These ensure the design is placed correctly on top.
- Read the instructions for Machine Quilting on page 162 and set the machine accordingly.

### CUTTING
#### MUSLIN
- Cut a large square 64–66 in.

#### RED FLANNEL
- Cut one 15½ in. square.
- Cut four squares each 3½ in.
- For binding cut strips 1¼ in., wide to total 250 in. when joined.

#### DARK TEAL BLUE
- Cut two squares each 16 × 16 in. and divide each once diagonally.
- Cut eight 3½-in. squares.

#### FLANNEL PRINT
- Cut two borders each 36½ × 9½ in. and two borders each 54½ × 9½ in.

#### PLAIDS/STRIPES
- From one plaid or stripe, cut four strips each 15½ × 3½ in. for inner frame.
- From a different plaid or stripe cut four strips each 30½ × 3½ in. for second frame.
- Cut a total of seventy-two 3½ in. squares from a mix of all the fabrics for the outer border.

**164**  INSTANT EXPERT: **QUILTING**

## Sewing

1 Prepare backing and batting with center lines, as directed opposite. Set machine as directed, with an even-feed or walking foot if available. Work with ¼-in. seam allowances.

2 Center the red flannel square on point, right side up, and baste.

3 Place two inner framing strips, right side down with raw edges level, on two opposite sides of the center square and pin or baste. Machine stitch through all layers. Neaten the threads as you work.

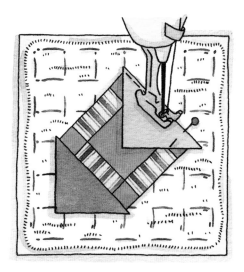

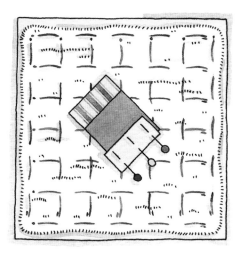

4 Turn the framing strips right side up and finger-press the seam. Pin or baste the outer edges to the backing layers. Each time you add a unit, repeat this step before adding the next.

5 Sew one red 3½-in. square to each end of the remaining inner framing strips, then press. Place the assembled strips, right side down and raw edges level, on the remaining two sides of the center square, matching corner square seams to existing frame, and sew through all layers.

6 Place the long side of one dark teal triangle right side down with raw edges level on one side of the framed center. Pin or baste, taking care not to stretch the bias edge, then sew. Repeat on the opposite side. Then add triangles to the remaining two opposite sides. These may come up slightly oversized so true up if required before proceeding.

7 Repeat steps 3–5 to add the second outer frame, with dark teal corner squares instead of red ones, around the center.

8 Place short print borders on opposite sides of the framed center using the same method. Then add the long print borders to the remaining two sides.

9 Using the 3½-in. squares randomly, assemble four outer borders of 18 squares. Add a dark teal corner square at both ends of two borders.

10 Sew the short borders to opposite sides of the quilt. Then add the longer borders, matching seams of the corner squares to the existing border seam.

11 Baste around the quilt within the seam allowance and trim excess batting and backing.

12 Join the binding strips and attach to the quilt following the instructions on pages 48–52. The binding is cut to allow ease for the thickness of the flannel fabrics.

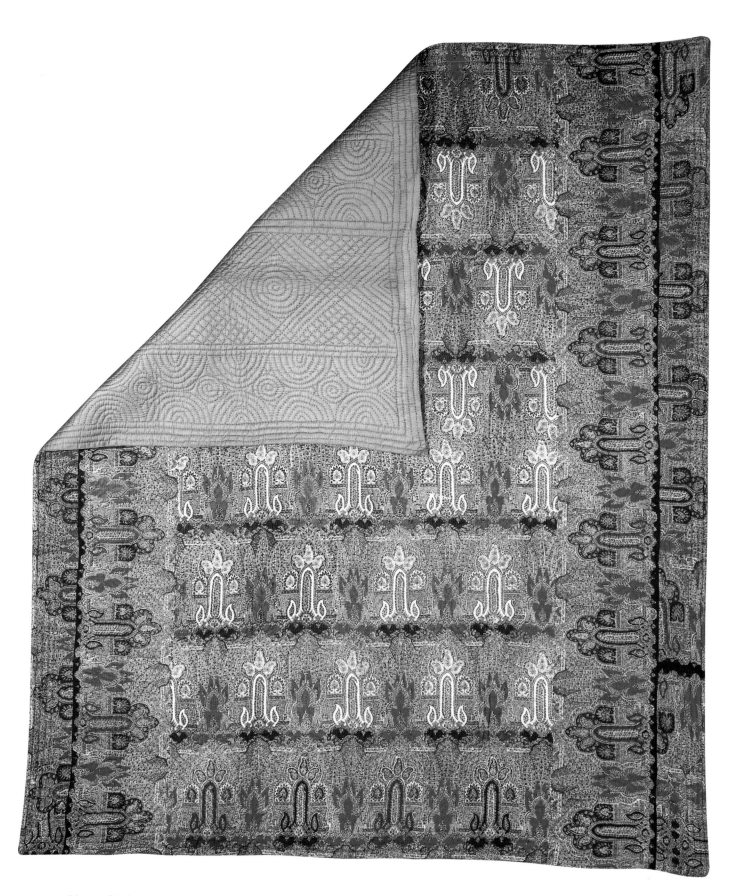

**Above:** Paisley wholecloth, English, ca.1900.

# HAND QUILTING

The quilting stitch is a simple one. The challenge is to work it with small, evenly-sized stitches and spaces with the same appearance on both sides. Beginners should aim for straight, even stitches. With practice, the size of the stitch can be reduced. It is useful to know that the size of any stitching will be affected by the weight of fabric and the texture of batting, no matter how experienced the quilter. So expect some variation on different projects.

## Quilting

① Cut a 15- to 18-inch length of quilting thread. If it is not a prewaxed thread, draw it across a piece of wax. Waxing helps the thread to glide through the quilt layers.

② Thread the needle and make a small knot at one end. To make the knot, wind the thread around your forefinger and then pass the needle alongside the fingernail through the loop as illustrated. Pull the knot firmly into position at the end of the thread.

③ Start quilting from the center and work outward.

④ To hide the knot in the batting, insert the point of the needle into the quilt top a short distance away from where you wish to start sewing and run the needle into the batting without going through to the backing. Bring the needle out where you wish to start and pull the thread until the knot stops on the quilt top. Give it a slight tug to "pop" the knot through the top to the inside of the quilt.

⑤ Work running stitches through all layers. To get them even, insert the needle vertically through all layers, then direct it forward and up to the top of the work. This also helps reduce the amount of drifting that can occur between the three layers when one layer is pushed more than the others.

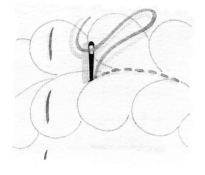

⑥ To keep the reverse of the quilt looking neat, the ends of thread must be finished off. Make a small backstitch, splitting the previous stitch to anchor it. Then insert the needle through the layers without going through to the back and come out a short distance away, if possible along where the line of stitching will continue, because this will help secure it. Keep a very slight tension on the thread as you carefully cut it close to the surface and the end will slip back inside the layers.

A quick and undetectable alternative is to make a knot in the thread and hide it in the batting. The instructions are lengthy, but in fact it is easy to do (see page 168).

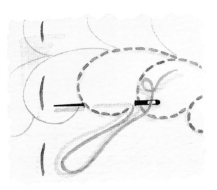

## Making Knots to Tie Off Quilting

**1** To get the knot in the correct position on the thread, lay the thread on the quilt in the direction in which your final stitch will be. Keep it in place with your left thumb (if right-handed).

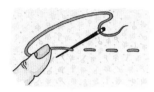

**fig. 1**

**2** Slip the needle under the thread and rotate the needle over the thread and back under it. Put the point of the needle into the fabric in the right place to complete the last stitch, passing the needle into the batting only.

**fig. 2**

**3** With the left thumb keeping the coil close to the quilt's surface, bring the needle out to the top of the work and pull through carefully. The knot should form tightly around the thread at just the correct point. As it reaches the fabric, a tiny tug will pop it into the batting with the last stitch perfectly in place. Hold the thread firmly as you snip to encourage the tail to slip inside the batting.

**fig. 3**

## Rocking the Needle
Many quilters find they need a second thimble on the finger beneath the work that directs the needle forward. Use the fingers below to push against the layers, slightly compressing the batting as the needle is pushed in and down. This makes it easier to get the needle back through to the top. Coordinating this action produces the rocking action described by many experienced quilters. With practice, the needle can be rocked to pick up a series of stitches on the needle before the thread is drawn through them all at once.

## Stab-stitch Quilting
An alternative way to quilt is to use a stab-stitch rather than a true running stitch. Although the appearance is the same, stab-stitching requires two steps to make a single stitch and for this reason is thought to be slower.

To stab-stitch, position your preferred hand beneath the quilt because it will be easier to control when you cannot see it. Holding the needle in your other hand, insert it through the quilt layers, catch it with the hand below, and push it back to the top of the work.

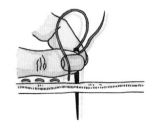

**fig. 1**

**fig. 2**

**Above:** Wholecloth quilt, by Linda Maltman, English, twentieth century.

**Above:** Detail of a hand-stitched quilt top, by Gisela Thwaites.

**Above:** Detail showing the intricate quilting on the quilt back.

# HAND QUILTING—SASHIKO QUILTING

The Japanese word *sashiko* refers to both the stitching and the grid-like patterns identified with the technique. It is worked over two layers of indigo-dyed cloth without batting and was originally used to strengthen workmen's jackets. The stitches, worked in a heavy white thread, are about twice the size of the spaces between them.

You can buy sashiko thread from quilting suppliers, or you can use coton à broder, cotton pearl, silk buttonhole twist, and some grades of crochet cotton. Because very long threads are used, and the thread is pulled through the fabric many times, a twisted thread is needed. Stranded threads shred after a little while. The size of needle you use will be partly determined by the thread you select. It is traditional to pick up a series of stitches onto the needle before drawing it through the cloth. This makes the stitching quicker to work but requires a long needle. Any type of design can be worked in sashiko-style quilting.

## Making a Sample Block

❶ Enlarge your design, either on a photocopier, taping together several sheets to make an area of the correct size, or by drawing it up on graph paper to the measurements given with each pattern.

❷ Mark the design on the right side of a 12-inch square of top fabric. Place over a second layer, wrong sides together, and baste.

❸ Using a running stitch, work the design in a logical way, either from the center out or from one end of the block to the other. A grid is usually worked by sewing one line of the pattern across the whole area to be quilted. Then the second line is worked and so on until the design is complete.

❹ Stitch size is often subtly adapted to fit the pattern being worked. However, good sashiko shows the same number of stitches on the same part of the design throughout. It is also necessary to adjust stitch size to turn corners because a corner can only be formed by the needle's entering or leaving the fabric. When multiple lines of a pattern meet, the preferred effect is to have a space at the center on all lines, with stitches radiating from it like the petals of a flower.

**Above:** Illustration of sashiko quilting.
**Right:** *Sashiko mini quilt*, by Eilean MacDonald, British, twentieth century.

# HAND QUILTING—TRAPUNTO

The idea of sewing an enclosed shape on two layers of fabric, then stuffing it with some kind of filling, goes back a long way. Some of the earliest surviving quilts feature this technique. Trapunto combines well with other quilting styles when the surrounding is quilted, such as with a regular filling pattern or a meandering or stippled texture. Take care not to overstuff the shapes or the work will warp. Also, overstuffed shapes are the first to display signs of wear during use, their taut covering becoming quite threadbare while the rest of the quilt may still be in good condition.

## Making a Trapunto Sample Design

1 From muslin, cut a square for the block top and mark with a design of enclosed shapes.

2 Cut a matching square of loosely woven fabric, such as cheesecloth or turban muslin. Place behind the muslin and baste together.

3 On the right side, by hand or by machine, quilt the drawn outlines.

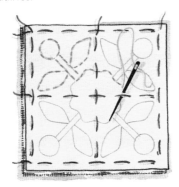

4 Turn to the back of the work to fill the shapes. If the backing is sufficiently loosely woven, you will be able to ease the threads open with a blunt knitting needle. Through the hole, insert tiny scraps of filling, such as batting or trapunto wool. When filled, tease the threads back into place.

5 If the backing is too firmly woven, cut a small opening in the shape and fill. Sew the opening closed as neatly as possible without reducing the area of the background excessively.

**Above:** Detail of *Princess Feather* with trapunto quilted berries and yellow circles, American, nineteenth century.

# TYING AND SEEDING

Tying is a traditional way to secure the layers of a quilt together, particularly one with a thick filling. Often called "comforters," these quilts were tied at quite large intervals, such as the corners or centers of blocks. The thread can add an accent of color when the tails are left long. Alternatively, the ties can be made inconspicuous and tied to the back and finished with a button.

Ties can be worked with narrow ribbon or with decorative embroidery thread and some knitting yarn. The only test is whether the yarn will travel through the quilt layers. If you want to include something too textured to pull through the layers easily, insert the textured yarn under the first stitch and then tie all ends together. Ties with extra strands added to them for more volume are called "tufts."

## Making Ties and Tufts

❶ Use a darning needle and a length of pearl cotton or crochet cotton. Ties can be worked with a double strand or more of thread. If threading several strands through, these can be a mixture of colors.

❷ Make a stitch through all layers where the tie will be (fig. 1). Then make a second stitch at the same place and use a square knot to fasten the ends (fig. 2 and fig. 3). After working all the ties, trim the ends to the desired length.

❸ For speed and convenience, ties may be worked consecutively. Put a long length of doubled thread in the needle. Start where the first tie will be with the basic two stitches. With the thread still attached, move to the next place and make two stitches. Continue in the same way until the thread is used. Make sure there is enough length left between ties for tying the knots (fig. 4). Take care not to draw up the quilt as the thread is carried from one tie to the next. Snip the thread between the stitches and tie the ends in the usual way with a square knot.

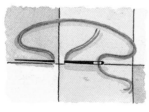

**fig. 1**

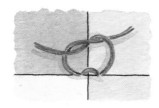

**fig. 2**

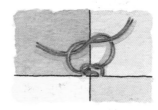

**fig. 3**

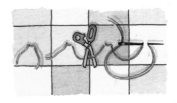

**fig. 4**

## Seeding

Seeding is related to tying, although it might be considered more an embroidery stitch than a quilting one. It combines well with tying, anchoring the layers at regular intervals like ties but with a less noticeable appearance.

To make a seed stitch, work two small stitches next to each other, then pass the needle through the batting, bringing it out where you will place the next seed. The maximum distance between seeds is determined by the length of the needle.

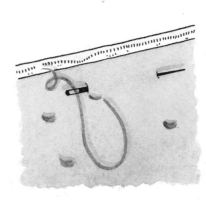

**Left:** Detail of embroidered crazy quilt, American, early twentieth century.

# TEMPLATES

The following templates need to be enlarged as directed
to the distance indicated between the red dots.

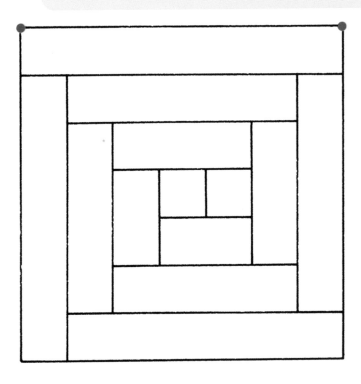

Log Cabin, page 93, enlarge to 7 inches between red dots.

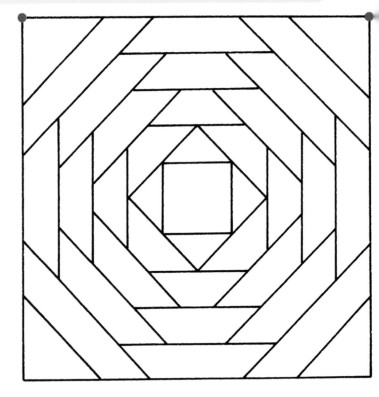

Pineapple Log Cabin, page 96, enlarge to 7½ inches between red dots.

Turtledove, page 154, enlarge to 10 inches between red dots.

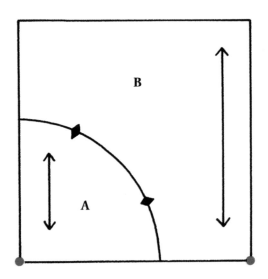

Drunkard's Path Block, page 87, enlarge to 5 inches between red dots.

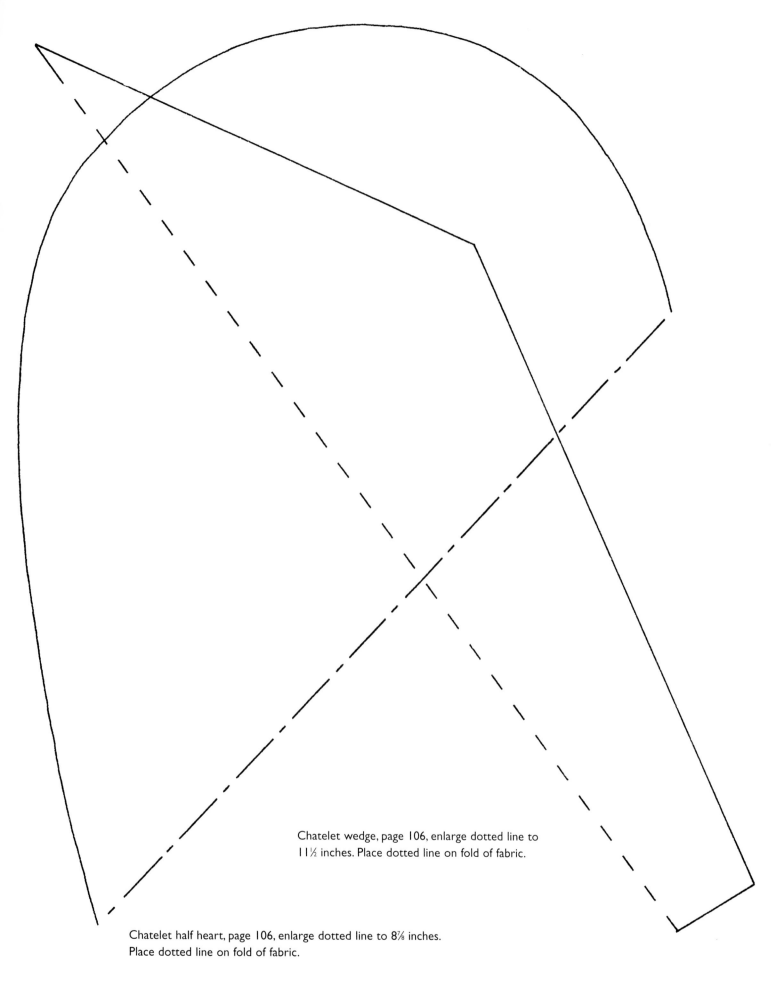

Chatelet wedge, page 106, enlarge dotted line to
11½ inches. Place dotted line on fold of fabric.

Chatelet half heart, page 106, enlarge dotted line to 8⅞ inches.
Place dotted line on fold of fabric.

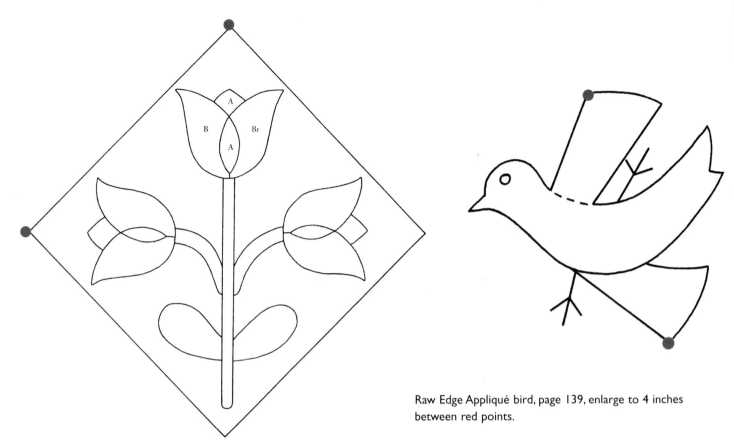

Tulip wall hanging block, page 137, enlarge to 5 inches between red dots.

Raw Edge Appliqué bird, page 139, enlarge to 4 inches between red points.

Raw Edge Appliqué Holly leaf, page 139, enlarge until leaf is 1½ inches long.

Mola Wall Hanging cat, page 152, enlarge to 2⅜ inches between red points.

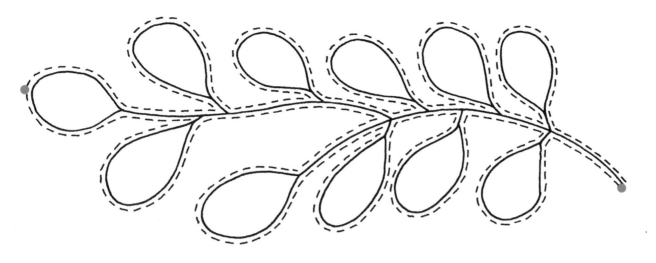

**Above:** Mola Wall Hanging leaf, page 152, enlarge to 10 inches between red points.

**Below:** Mola Wall Hanging cat, page 152, enlarge to 6 inches between red points.

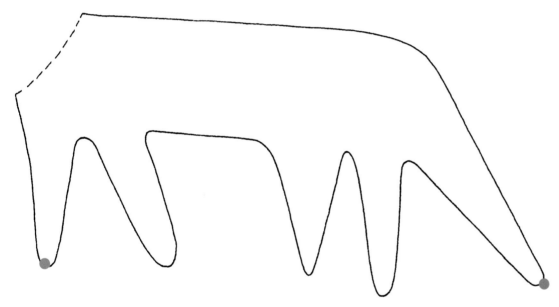

**Below Left:** Mola Wall Hanging cat, page 152, enlarge to 4⅜ inches between red points.

**Below:** Mola Wall Hanging cat, page 152, enlarge to 3⅝ inches between red points.

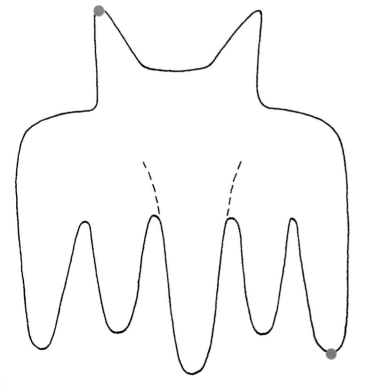

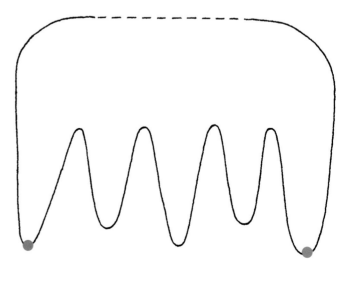

Baltimore Basket quilt, lower left of basket, page 140, enlarge to 3¾ inches between red points.

**Left:** Baltimore Basket quilt, ribbon tails, page 140, enlarge to 6 inches between red points.
**Right:** Baltimore Basket quilt, lower right of basket, page 140, enlarge to 2 inches between red points.

**Below:** Baltimore Basket quilt, lower right of basket, page 140, enlarge to 2 inches between red points.

**Above:** Baltimore Basket quilt, garland, page 140, enlarge to 10½ inches between red points.

Baltimore Basket quilt, top right of basket, page 140, enlarge to 3⅛ inches between red points.

Left: Baltimore Basket quilt, Corner garland, page 140, enlarge to 10½ inches between red points.
Below: Baltimore Basket quilt, bow, page 140, enlarge to 4⅝ inches between red points.

Baltimore Basket quilt, ribbon border, page 140, enlarge to 5½ inches between red points.

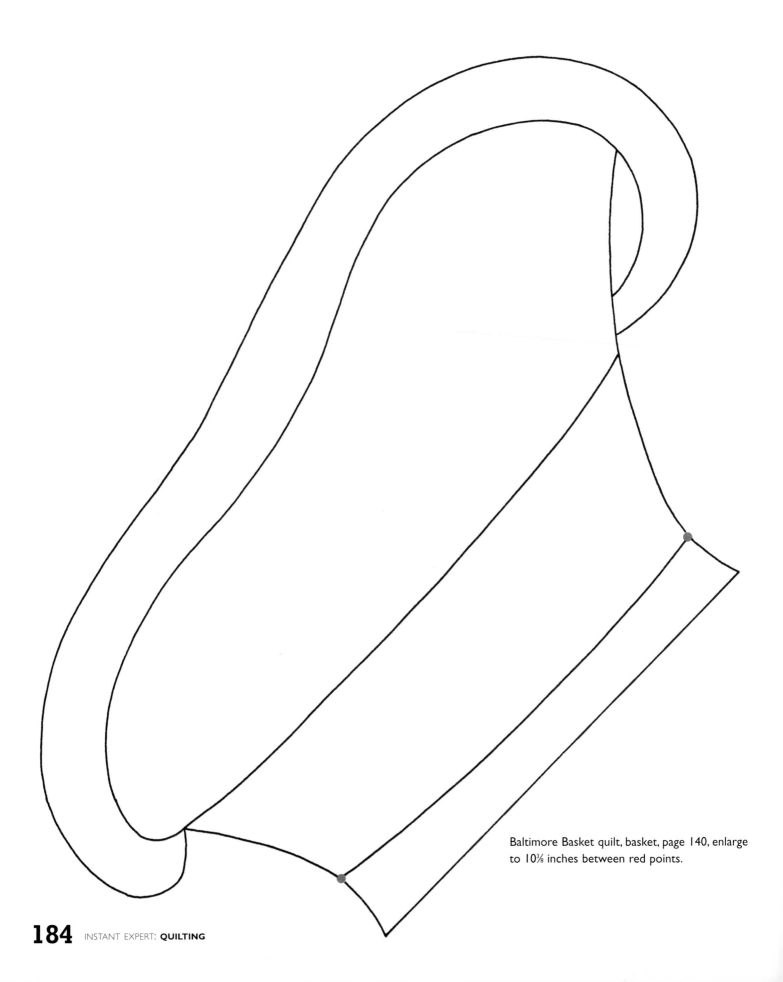

Baltimore Basket quilt, basket, page 140, enlarge to 10⅜ inches between red points.

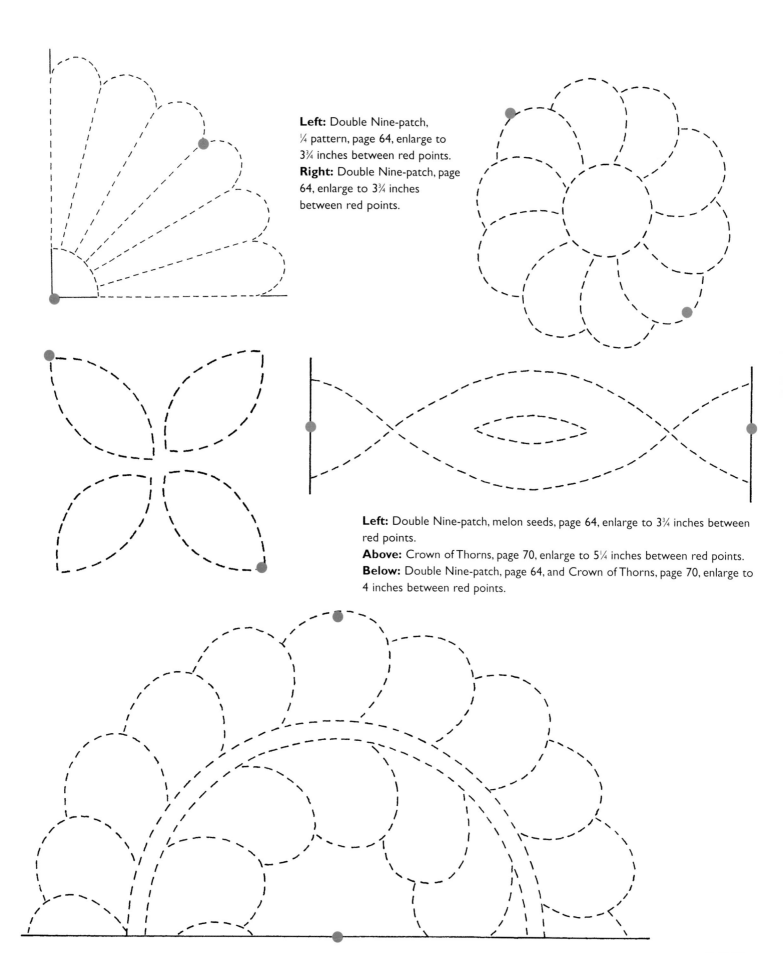

**Left:** Double Nine-patch, ¼ pattern, page 64, enlarge to 3¾ inches between red points.
**Right:** Double Nine-patch, page 64, enlarge to 3¾ inches between red points.

**Left:** Double Nine-patch, melon seeds, page 64, enlarge to 3¾ inches between red points.
**Above:** Crown of Thorns, page 70, enlarge to 5¼ inches between red points.
**Below:** Double Nine-patch, page 64, and Crown of Thorns, page 70, enlarge to 4 inches between red points.

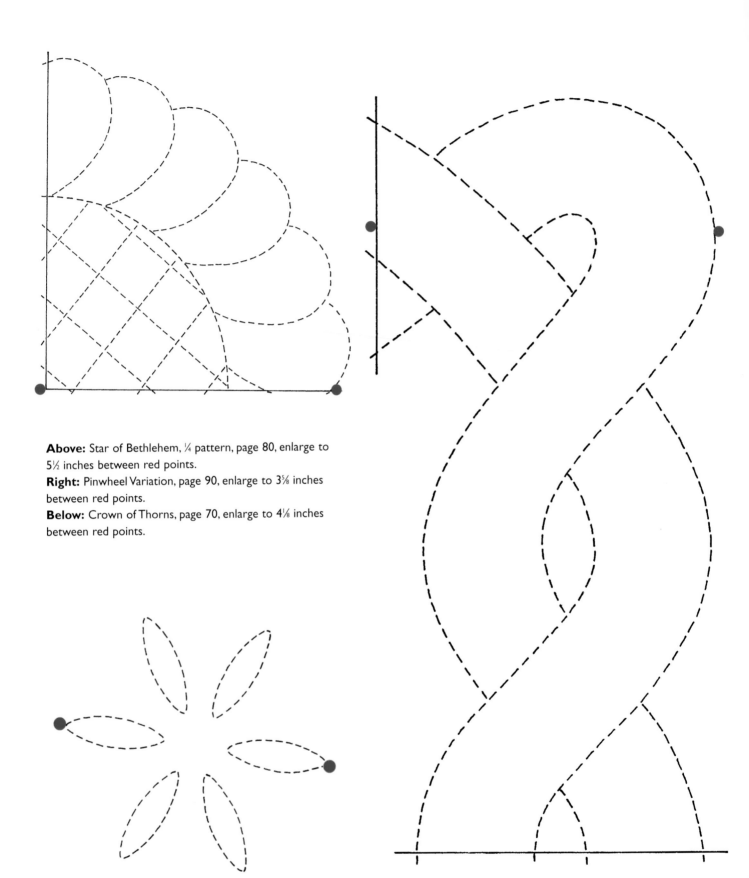

**Above:** Star of Bethlehem, ¼ pattern, page 80, enlarge to 5½ inches between red points.

**Right:** Pinwheel Variation, page 90, enlarge to 3⅝ inches between red points.

**Below:** Crown of Thorns, page 70, enlarge to 4⅛ inches between red points.

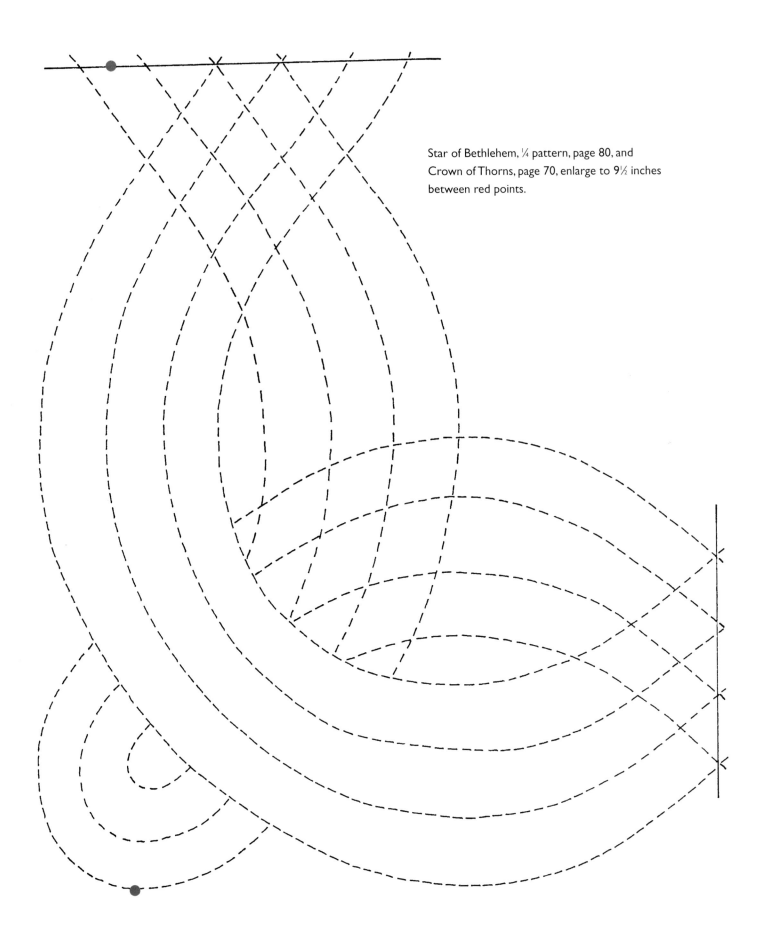

Star of Bethlehem, ¼ pattern, page 80, and
Crown of Thorns, page 70, enlarge to 9½ inches
between red points.

Black-and-White Optical-Illusion quilt, page 126, the shaded areas represent the white-on-white strip-pieced fabrics.

Pinwheel Variation, page 90, enlarge to 6 inches between red points.

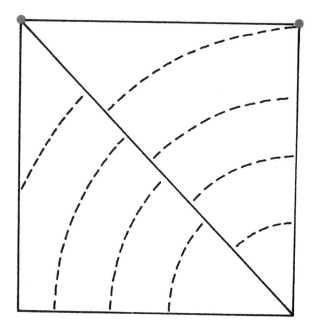

# ABOUT THE AUTHOR

**Jenni Dobson** studied at art colleges in Coventry and Manchester in England in the 1960s, eventually specializing in textiles. In 1968, she started as an adult education tutor teaching pattern-cutting and dressmaking, and took various tutor-training courses, eventually gaining a post-graduate diploma in adult education in 1983.

Dobson first began freelance writing for adult education journals. After her youngest child started school, she worked, part-time at first, for an audio-visual and video company, initially creating artwork but extending into designing, writing, and directing program-making for training and promotional purposes. At the same time, Dobson was still a part-time evening class tutor with interests shifting toward patchwork and quilting in the late 1970s.

After about seven to eight years working with the audio-visual company, Dobson decided to try fulfilling her own ambitions and applied herself to quiltmaking full-time and, as they say, hasn't looked back. In addition to her activities in the United Kingdom, she has had quilts exhibited in the United States, Europe, Japan, and Korea, besides teaching and speaking in the United States and Europe. Dobson is also a member of the British Quilt Study Group, a special interest section of the Quilters' Guild, and currently edits its newsletter. For the past two years, she has also been a tutor on the Quilt Judges distance learning program run by the Quilters' Guild of the British Isles.

Dobson has contributed to a number of magazines and appeared on both television and radio.

**Also by the Author:**

*Art Deco Quilts & How to Make them*, MQ Publications
*Sweet & Simple Country Quilts*, MQ Publications
*Readers' Digest Patchwork, Quilting & Appliqué*, MQ Publications

**Besides other books, Jenni has also contributed to:**

*Patchwork & Quilting*, the British magazine
*Popular Patchwork*, a British magazine
*The Quilter*, the magazine of the Quilters' Guild of the British Isles
*Patchwork Quilt Tsushin*, Japan

Visit Jenni at www.jennidobson.co.uk

# INDEX

## Picture Credits

Page 12: © Copyright of The Quilters' Guild of the British Isles. Page 55 and 57: Jenni Dobson. Page 189: Alix Ashurst.